THE END OF WORK

The End of Work

As We Know It

**The Commonsense Guide to America's
Workplace Revolution**

*Nadine Mockler & Laurie Young
With Arlene Matthews*

Writers Club Press
San Jose   New York   Lincoln   Shanghai

The End of Work
As We Know It

Writers Club Press
an imprint of iUniverse, Inc.

For information address:
iUniverse, Inc.
5220 S. 16th St., Suite 200
Lincoln, NE 68512
www.iuniverse.com

ISBN: 0-595-21735-4

Printed in the United States of America

We dedicate this effort to our families — Bill, Elizabeth, Molly, Aaron, Andy, Travis, Taylor and Anna Grace — without whom Flexible Resources, Inc. would not be alive and flourishing. And to all of our clients, candidates and colleagues who continue to serve as inspiration and proof that thinking "outside the box" does indeed create a culture that brings out the best in all of us.

Contents

Preface

We were just putting the finishing touches on this book when everything changed on September 11, 2001.

Our business has always been about making the most of our lives by creating the most effective work/family balance possible. In the wake of the tragedy, the desire for more time — for family and what matters most — is more urgent than ever.

The purpose of *The End of Work As We Know It* is to make the actual concept of work make sense for the world we live in today, and to help businesses cope successfully with the blurring lines between work and family. It's an instruction manual for giving people the time they crave, creating effective employees who in turn will give companies the focus, energy and high productivity necessary for future success and survival.

It also explains how the relentlessly forward motion of technology and the movement toward a decentralized workplace, coupled with new beliefs about how best to live our lives, are making current concepts of work obsolete.

If this book succeeds, businesses will come to view employees as a precious resource that flourishes in the right environment and employees will realize that work, which makes up one-third of our lives, can and should be fulfilling — not just a chore to be withstood until retirement. Indeed, as you will discover, even retirement is no longer what it used to be.

The End of Work is about the nature of work and how it must change to accommodate the new nature of things. Work is an essential part of our lives and should be embraced. The following is a commonsense guide to making that happen.

A Word of Introduction

The two of us met in the mid-1980s when we were advertising executives at Della Femina, McNamee WCRS. We met again a few years later, after we had the first of our children and were "put out to pasture" in the suburbs.

Although we both wanted to spend time with our families, we were also eager to continue working. With no business "track" available to us other than the usual full-time, full-speed-ahead, we decided to start a business of our own — one that would solve a huge problem for people like ourselves.

In 1989, we created Flexible Resources, Inc., a full-service staffing and consulting firm providing non-traditional employment solutions. For more than a decade, we have actively participated in creating a flexible workplace at hundreds of corporations. Among our clients are Fortune 500 firms such as American Express, Cendant Mobility, GE Capital, JP Morgan Chase, Kraft, Mott's Corporation, PepsiCo, Playtex, Prodigy Services Co., United Technologies, and Unilever. The employees we place with these concerns are financial analysts, CFOs, accountants, human resource executives, engineers, product managers, lawyers, sales managers, technical writers, IT specialists, and account executives, among many others.

We started Flexible Resources because it was practical; we didn't realize that it was also prescient.

At first we were thought of as "the mommy-track company." Then the recession of the early 1990s hit, and our company's image changed. American corporations still needed good people — better people than ever, in fact — but the bottom line was critical. Suddenly everyone discovered that hiring qualified employees who desired something other than conventional employment opportunities also made sound economic sense. An entire pool of talent that might have been ignored was now in high demand, and Flexible Resources became the "cost-effective staffing company."

Then — as it is wont to do — the economy changed again. With unemployment at an all-time low, companies found that the best way to attract and retain top talent was to offer flexibility. Again we were there to pair talent with opportunity.

And today? Today we find ourselves riding the crest of the wave of the future. By the turn of the millennium, virtually every business publication and trend-tracker had predicted a stunning rise in flexible work arrangements across the board, noting that these would be here to stay. We wondered what took them so long to reach this conclusion.

But no matter. At this point there are few workplace watchers who would disagree. Flexible work arrangements — sane, humane, productive and profitable alternatives — are at the heart of the current zeitgeist. Our workforce will demand them. Our businesses will realize how much they can prosper from them. Our technology, now on the verge of complete preparedness, will completely accommodate them. A good thing, too, because our global 24/7 economy has rendered the 9-to-5 work model obsolete.

Of course, the many changes involved will not occur without accompanying angst. As an old adage correctly advises us, "People change when the pain of changing is less than the pain of not changing." The tipping moment when that balance shifts irrevocably is right on the horizon. Traditional work schedules, seemingly innocuous enough, have contributed to a plethora of fiscal, societal and psychological problems. Only non-traditional work options can help alleviate those problems.

We don't mean to imply that unconventional work arrangements offer a total social, economic or personal panacea. Like all departures from the status quo, "the end of work as we know it" will create challenges that require innovative solutions. Indeed, these potential challenges are among the key reasons that we have written this book.

In the first of three sections, *The End of Work As We Know It* offers an overview of where we stand now in the workplace, outlining both inherent problems and soon-to-be-realized solutions. In the second section, we offer guidelines and suggestions for employees undergoing the shift to increased flexibility — and hence increased autonomy and personal responsibility. In the third section, we provide effective and innovative strategies for those that already or will soon manage the flexible workplace, be they top executives or mid-level managers in a large corporation, or start-up entrepreneurs building the future by leveraging the power of flexibility.

While we don't pretend to have all the answers, we have served on the front lines of the struggle toward a flexible workplace for many years. We have identified what we believe to be the best practices for all concerned, and we have suggestions for how to develop continuing good practices as the New Workplace evolves.

So while you won't find a panacea herein, you will find promise. It's a promise that can and will be fulfilled as America embraces a new balance in work, and in life.

Nadine Mockler
Laurie Young
Greenwich, Connecticut
March 2002

PART I

The Workplace Is Revolting

"Organization has been made by man;
It can be changed by man."

—William H. Whyte, Jr,
The Organization Man

1

Why Work Doesn't Work

Let's say that when you go to bed tonight you fall under the influence of an enchanted sleeping spell — or, for Star Trek fans, into the vortex of a space-time anomaly. In either case, you wake up the "next" morning alert and refreshed, only to learn from the date on the morning paper that five years have elapsed while you dozed.

Because the paper also tells you it's Monday, you realize that — anomalies or no — it's time to get to the office. So, after kissing the family good-bye (my, the children have grown) you proceed with your usual routine. Sighing at the thought of your usual 20-mile, 45-minute rush-hour commute, you steer your car up a twisty "on" ramp and out into traffic.

Except that there isn't any traffic, to speak of. There are other cars, to be sure, but they are moving steadily along at the speed limit and the view from the top of the first hill's crest reveals a startling lack of bottlenecks ahead. You can't figure it out. Was a new national holiday declared during your extended nap?

At the office, your consternation continues. It's 8 a.m. Where are all your co-workers? Some are there, but many cubicles are unoccupied. Has there been a massive downsizing? Is your company going under? Since you brought your morning paper along, you flip to the stock quotes. Hmmm…actually, your company stock is way up. And here's an odd thing: Of your key competitors, one of them — Acme OmniServices — is no longer listed on the exchange.

Nothing about this makes any sense. What could have happened in the last five years? You feel lost. But just as you're becoming overwhelmed with questions and confusion, you spot your department manager, Bob, coming around the corner. Bob, a frenetic "Type A," always knows what's happening in every nook and cranny of your organization. He's the guy to give you the 411.

Perplexed, you query Bob about what could possibly be going on. As you do, a slow smile spreads across his lips. "Hey, you must be that hypothetical case. The one with the space-time whatchamacallit," he says calmly. (Funny, in general Bob seems a lot calmer than he used to, and he lacks those trademark circles under his eyes.)

"Well, yes," you confess. "I really need to come up to speed."

"Okey-doke," says Bob. What he tells you is that over the last five years your company was one of many that became a flexible workplace. Indeed, like the vast majority of companies in the Fortune 500, not to mention smaller organizations and start-up operations, it has embraced all sorts of non-traditional employment options. These, he explains, range from full-time work on a flexible or compressed schedule, to telecommuting, to permanent part-time or limited-term assignments, to innovative job shares — and various combinations thereof.

The chipper and unusually well-rested Bob elaborates. "That's why you didn't get snarled in a traffic jam on your way in," he says. "And that's why our stock is up, big-time. Our productivity is greater now, no matter what part of the economic cycle we're in. We're retaining top talent, too, and morale has never been higher."

"But what happened to Acme OmniServices?" you ask, mentioning your main corporate rival. "They were cleaning our clock in all kinds of markets."

"Kaput," intones Bob. "As our CEO said years ago, when it comes to the flexibility mandate there are only two kinds of companies — the quick and the dead."

This is a lot to absorb, and your head is reeling. Still, all of it sounds pretty good so far. Can it be for real? Maybe you'll find out more at the

Monday morning staff meeting, you think, so you ask Bob if it's in Conference Room B as usual.

But Bob tells you that they haven't had those dreadful Monday morning meetings for years. "You won't miss them will you? All that grandstanding and brown-nosing. What a bore. Hey, remember the time Sheila started nodding off and Mike actually started snoring? Steve's forecasting report just did them in!"

Ah, memories. You recall how many times you, too, came close to lapsing into a coma during Steve's long-winded soliloquies.

But still, if there's no staff meeting, how are you going to catch up on all the fine points you need to get re-oriented? Maybe Linda, your trusty department administrator, can help.

"What time does Linda come in?" you ask.

"Well," Bob replies, "on Mondays she doesn't come in. She requested a job-share arrangement nearly five years ago, back when I admit I still needed quite a bit of convincing. We'd never want to lose her, though, so we found someone to match her up with. His name's Ben. Goes to grad school part-time and works Monday through Wednesday. Linda comes in Wednesday through Friday. They're like peanut butter and jelly, those two. I tell you, things have never run more smoothly.

"So, if you need anything at all today, Ben will help you out. He can also show you how to download that forecasting report and read it for yourself," Bob adds with a wink. "Have a great day!"

❖   ❖   ❖   ❖   ❖

We call the preceding our story of Rip Van Worker.

But it's not a fairy tale or a sci-fi scenario. <u>It is what the future will look like</u>. For real.

Data from the 1997 Census supplement showed that in 1989, 11.9 percent of the American population worked on some sort of flexible schedule. By 1997 that number had risen to 27.6 percent, nearly equally distributed between men and women.[1] Of course, that meant nearly three-quarters of the working population was still mired in <u>in</u>flexible employment situations. Yet — based on the sheer power of demographics, the relentless thrust of technology and the realities of global business — we predict that within the next five years these numbers will shift radically. <u>By then, more than three-quarters of the employed population will have a</u> <u>significant degree of flexibility on the job</u>.

Of course, none of us are going to nod off for the next five years and wake up with the transitional period behind us. We're all going to witness the change, participate in it — and, indeed, create it as we go.

This will be a challenge, to be sure, but one well worth rising to. For the benefits we reap, as individuals and as a society, will be unparalleled. Meanwhile, the perils of hanging on to the status quo loom large.

In this book, we'll offer a roadmap for the journey, along with strategies for minimizing some of the inevitable discomfort and disorientation that accompany a major shift in our way of thinking. But before we discuss work as it will be, let's look at how the majority of us still work today, and why that doesn't work anymore.

Work as we know it

The way we work today — up and out early in the morning and bound for home at dinnertime (more or less) — is a model dating from the Industrial Revolution. The socioeconomic changes that occurred in the late 18th century, when we switched from home-based hand production to factory manufacturing, resulted in people working outside the home from dawn to dusk, six days a week (with Sunday as the only day of rest). Granted, we have managed to trim the 18th century grind somewhat. Yet despite the myriad contemporary miracles of technology that can connect members of the workforce anytime, anywhere, the rules governing where and when we work remain antiquated.

Today, the vast majority of us still face a work schedule defined by terms that describe how we feel about it: Blue Monday (here we go again), Hump Day (we're halfway done), and TGIF (at last!). The typical work-week is structured so that we start out full-throttle, powered by nervous energy mixed with dread; sputter toward burnout mode by midweek; and veer toward half-giddy, half-guilty procrastination on Friday. Then we head into a two-day weekend, overwhelmed by all the necessary personal and family errands we've been unable to deal with before.

But what of the tasks and obligations that simply can't be accomplished on weekends? What about the car that needs to be inspected before you get another citation or that ancient tooth filling your dentist said must be replaced? What about the first grade's "Pageant of Fruits and Vegetables," not so conveniently scheduled for a weekday morning, in which your child is debuting as a brussel sprout? In the non-flexible workplace, one's choices in such situations are severely limited. One either becomes a motor-vehicle scofflaw with bad dental hygiene and a child badly in need of psychotherapy, or one is forced to sneak around and concoct excuses.

Not long ago we were struck by an anecdote recounted by Michael Lewis in his book, *The New New Thing: A Silicon Valley Story*. In it, the author describes a long, intense meeting between some heavy-hitter Internet entrepreneurs and a group of Wall Street bankers. In the center of the conference table, around which participants scrutinized an elaborate bubble chart and discussed huge sums of money, was a black squawk box. One of the bankers, a woman who had "called in sick," was listening by speakerphone. Lewis writes:

From time to time a squeak or gurgle emanated from the box at the center of the conference table. A baby! The woman…was holding a baby and the baby was refusing to keep quiet. Each time it mewled, the room used it as an excuse to depart from the Chart of Many Bubbles and share a hearty laugh…

"Gibagibagibagiba," went the baby.

"Ho, ho, ho," went all the people in the room.[2]

What was so funny? Partly it was the baby's endearing commentary — which no doubt helped relieve nervous tension. But partly it was the tacit understanding of everyone in the room as to what "calling in sick" really means.

There are times when no amount of creative truth-stretching can serve to reconcile the imbalance between work and "real life." As a result, real life often goes by the boards. We know employees who have been advised by bosses that missing their kids' graduations or siblings' wedding rehearsals, deferring visits to sick parents, or even delaying their honeymoon plans, was in their own best interests. (That is, if they considered keeping their jobs to be in their best interests).

We don't mean to insinuate that everyone works for such Simon Legree-type taskmasters. Indeed, most bosses have a high degree of empathy for time-strapped workers. Why shouldn't they? They have their own logistical problems trying to juggle the demands of work and life. Like everyone else, they have kids, spouses, siblings and parents, not to mention automobiles, appliances, homes and human bodies that require maintenance — and not always on a convenient schedule.

It is the traditional work-scheduling system that is the key culprit here. Put in place over 200 years ago, it has created habitual expectations that are impractical, unrealistic and — most important — utterly unnecessary in today's world. When we as a society alter the system we will, *ipso facto*, eliminate a goodly number of its absurdities and abuses.

The economy as we know it

If the traditional system makes little sense in the microcosm of the daily workplace, it makes even less sense in terms of the macrocosm of the overall economy.

As everyone knows, although some periodically attempt to deny, the economy is cyclical and always will be. As the "invisible hand" — as Adam Smith referred to it — directs and redirects the economy via the free market, things change. Then they change again.

When we began researching this book, for example, the American unemployment rate was at a 30-year low of less than 4 percent. The Dow Jones and Nasdaq were soaring. Correspondingly, there was universal dread that something or other would come along to apply brakes to our turbo-charged boom period. There were dire prognostications, some of which proved correct.

In this particular instance, the dot-coms bombed, venture capital dried up and the fallout for high-tech companies was severe. And then September 11th happened. But even if that cataclysm had not occurred, our white-hot economy was already cooling off.

Just as summer ultimately turns to winter, the economy cycles up and cycles back down. There is no business model possible that will eliminate this truth. Yet these severe economic swings could be profoundly mitigated — but for old habits.

Another upturn in our economy is, of course, in the cards sooner or later — as is another downturn. When the inevitable slowdowns unfold, some companies will continue to behave as if the only possible response, in terms of their workforce, is equally inevitable. That is, they will mandate drastic employee cutbacks and eliminate vast numbers of jobs.

Such actions, alas, force the economy into a deeper downward spiral. What's more, that kind of impulsive and poorly thought-out strategy leaves companies little leverage when the economic tide turns again. After each recession, many major firms discover their massive layoffs have hurt them badly. Frustrated customers, so under-serviced they felt virtually abandoned, have jumped ship, and the bottom line shows it. When these companies begin to rehire, some of them still won't assimilate the lessons they should have learned. They will attempt to rehire on reduced budgets, attracting only inexperienced college graduates. Thus, even after the overall economic picture improves it can take years to recover from the loss of talented, experienced personnel. Indeed, some organizations never will recover. They will lose their edge — or, more accurately, thoughtlessly relinquish it — permanently.

For companies that meet the next economic swing still mired in the outdated model of a 9-to-5 workforce, such negative reactivity will likely culminate in even swifter disaster, as the marketplace grows increasingly competitive. By over-reacting to an economic challenge, they will be like hapless drivers on icy roads — the kind that attempt to cope with a skid by trying to veer out of it, as opposed to gently steering into it and so regaining control.

For companies faced with the pressures of recession and/or inflation, gently steering into the skid consists of a simple, proactive solution: offering flexible options in lieu of layoffs. For example, instead of relieving 20,000 employees of their jobs, ask how many members of a company's workforce would like to remain on board on some sort of flexible part-time basis. Based on our research and experience, we predict the response would be overwhelmingly positive. In fact, we feel secure in predicting that large numbers of workers would be overjoyed.

Such a strategy allows an organization to hold on to its best people in hard times. Consequently they will retain their competitive edge, induce employee loyalty and keep their customers happy. Best of all, they will be in a superior position when the time comes to rev up operations again.

Like steering into a skid, this is not just a sensible solution, but potentially, nothing less than a life-saving one. Only so far we have not been sensible.

The journey as we know it

As long as we concluded our last point with a driving analogy, let's stay on the road for a moment and discuss another consequence of work as we know it.

You'll note that the first significant — and delightful — change our hypothetical time-traveler noticed with regard to his workday was the absence of the usual horrendous rush-hour traffic he had typically endured. We can hardly wonder at his resulting awe. When he nodded off, he — like the rest of us — would have been in the midst of dramatically worsening traffic conditions.

The Industrial Revolution at first forced the population to move to the cities. But, as the result of automobiles and a higher standard of living, huge numbers of us later migrated to family-friendly suburbs that were located long distances from our place of business. The result, according to the Federal Highway Commission, is that each of us, on average, spends about an hour and 13 minutes a day driving a car — chiefly to work. Since 1970, miles driven in the U.S.A. have nearly doubled, rising four times as fast as the growth of the population. The number of licensed drivers has also grown — by more than 60 percent — and the number of registered vehicles has nearly doubled.

Meanwhile, where are the new roadways to accommodate this lemming-like profusion of driving commuters? Well…pretty much nowhere. Between 1979 and 1997, the total miles of road grew by just 6 percent. In other words mileage driven grew 18 times faster than the highways and byways on which to log those miles.

Not surprisingly, traffic has become a "time-suck" of epic proportions. In New York, for example, some 2.1 million person-hours per year are lost to traffic delay. In Los Angeles, the figure is 2.3 million and rising. But lost time is not the only effect.

Herds of cars — bound for gridlock and spillback and all sorts of ominous-sounding traffic traps that result from this level of saturation — also punish the environment. What's more, driving is by far the most dangerous daily activity that most of us pursue. Traffic accidents are the leading cause of death for Americans under 40. In the words of Stephanie Faul, communications director for the AAA Foundation for Traffic Safety, "In

[this] century we seemed mostly to have banished death. The real risk is on the road." [3]

Sleep as we know it (or rather, don't know it)

One might suspect we would all be better, safer drivers if we were better rested. That suspicion has been borne out statistically. Each April, when we "spring ahead" into Daylight Savings Time and pare an hour of shut-eye from our nightly regime, there is a significant rise — some put it as high as 6 percent — in car crashes and accidental deaths of all kinds. [4]Compound this little detail with the fact that, according to the National Sleep Foundation, our average sleep-time as a nation has dropped by 20 percent over the past century, and we are left with a truly frightening scenario.

Yet, like the needless traffic jams we persist in creating out of habit, our chronic sleep-deprived "zombie" mode is one that can be addressed by a relatively simple solution. Let's each ask ourselves how much later each morning would we set our alarms if we were able to begin our workday at a later hour or work from home? Would we even need alarm clocks? (Sleep experts say the very presence of clocks by our bedsides indicates we are sleep-deprived, since we should be waking naturally refreshed at the end of a normal sleep cycle.)

How much sleep each of us needs may vary. We all seem to know people who routinely pop out of bed like freshly made toast after four hours, reinvigorated and raring to go. (Annoying, we know, but it takes all kinds.) Yet this natural variance is all the more reason why flexible schedules make sense.

Imagine a world where individuals can function optimally according to their natural rhythms and body clocks. How much better for them, how much better for business, and how much better for everyone that has to deal with them — on the road, on the job and at home.

Family life as we know it

Ah, home. This brings us to another topic that must be addressed with regard to the impact of work schedules. Work is where the money is — and, one hopes, the professional stimulation and fulfillment. But home is where the heart is, because home is where the family is.

We see no need to belabor the point that traditional work schedules too often play a part in undermining family harmony. This fact is blatantly obvious to anyone who works and who tries to maintain some semblance of intimacy with loved ones at home. Missing grade-school plays and pageants, not to mention those intramural track meets and Little League practices, is only the tip of the iceberg. We've all heard horror stories about kids parked in day care for 11 hours at a stretch. We've also heard about older "latchkey foundlings" left alone during critical after-school hours — a time when, say experts who study such things, they are more likely to get into trouble than at any other time of day. We know, often firsthand, about two-income couples who barely catch a passing glimpse of each other as they juggle their professional and domestic responsibilities.

Twenty years ago, society believed the best solution for working parents was to install day-care centers at the office. But that only meant companies felt justified in having parents work longer and longer hours. The result left more kids without one-on-one contact with adults, and created a corresponding decline in overall standards of behavior and academic achievement.

The corporate day-care phenomenon has often been called a Band-Aid solution — temporary and insufficient. We think this is a charitable description. Alas, even when intentions are the very best and the programs are thoughtfully and skillfully crafted, the results are often counterproductive. For working families, is it better than a poke in the eye with a sharp stick? Well, sure — but barely. Imagine if, instead of such so-called solutions, we could repair the work culture so that family life was not an automatic and universal casualty.

For most of human history, family life and work were intertwined, via hunting and gathering, farming, and craft skills that were passed down from generation to generation. After the Industrial Revolution, this mode of existence virtually vanished in the Western World. Now the trend has the potential of being reversed — via flexible work arrangements.

Is this a good thing? We defer to Harvard sociobiologist Edward O. Wilson. Musing about the future in a *Wall Street Journal* interview conducted at the turn of the millennium, the renowned author and professor called such non-traditional work options as telecommuting and teleconferencing, "the most heartening and healthful trends…in social evolution and cultural evolution." He added, "It is more like our species evolved. You can interweave your family and your contacts with business all through the day." [5]

Of course, we assume Wilson is not naïve — and, we assure you, we're not either — regarding the complexities and difficulties of family life. Indeed, we will devote a later chapter to managing the challenges of the aforementioned "interweaving" process. Still, if the new work culture can afford more and more families a greater range of options, the resulting change in households across the country, and in American culture as a whole, is bound to be profoundly beneficial.

Stress as we know it

To recap where we stand today with regard to how we work is to paint a sorry picture. Look at us: A nation of groggy road warriors, enslaved by clocks and buffeted by the fickle winds of the market cycle. As a result, we suffer professionally and personally.

For the individual worker, desperately trying to figure out how to please both management and family while battling fatigue, burnout and general job insecurity, these factors add up to one large cumulative effect: stress. And for companies whose employees suffer stress the bottom line suffers, as well.

The U.S. National Institute for Occupational Safety and Health tells us that stress is becoming the biggest reason for worker disability claims. Employees who report a high level of stress have 46 percent higher medical costs than do those who report low levels. One in every four workers between the ages of 25 and 44 report stress-induced nervous strain so severe it diminishes their job performance. What's more, 40 percent of worker turnover is due to job stress. Just imagine, then, all the money that could be saved not only on medical and disability claims, but also on mitigating lost productivity and the high costs of recruiting and training replacement staff.

What is the main reason for job stress? Not tight deadlines or irascible bosses, studies show. Instead, it is the feeling of loss of control. If there were a better way to reinstate that sense of control than to let an employee participate in decisions as to when, where and how he will work, it would be news to us. Based on feedback from the thousands of people we've worked with, flexibility is the key.

The good news is that key is about to be placed in the lock and turned, opening the gateway to a new way of work, and of life, for us all.

Toward restoring a balance

Today we stand on the verge of another Industrial Revolution. A radical workplace transformation will, in the very near future, completely alter the way we think about organizational life. The things that induced so much awe and disbelief in our Rip Van Worker time-traveler will become commonplace.

Already, many major companies have begun to train managers to respect and accommodate the reality that employees have lives outside of work. Some even offer incentives that reward managers who support flexibility. Are the executives who set such policies a bunch of Goody-Two-Shoes bleeding hearts who want to give away the store? On the contrary. They are among the shrewdest in the pantheon of all-time clever businesspeople.

As a working nation, we are in a state of fundamental disequilibrium. Those who work to restore balance will reap rich rewards — not because they are good (we have nothing against goodness; it's just not the issue here) but because they are adaptable.

As the next chapter will show, evolutionary forces in our society — forces that range from sweeping demographic changes to fundamental shifts in the way humans process information — are driving flexibility, and rendering the traditional workplace extinct. The most flexible among us will be the fittest, and the fittest will flourish.

On the face of it, shifting from traditional to non-traditional work arrangements may seem like a small thing. A nice thing, a convenient thing, a humane thing — but no big deal. But if it is a small thing, it is the sort of small thing upon which great things depend. As Charles Darwin wrote, "What a trifling difference must often determine which shall survive and which shall perish."

2

The New Work Culture: A Natural Adaptation

The work of Abraham Maslow, highly influential in the fields of both humanistic psychology and management, offers a theory called the hierarchy of needs. This theory posits that human needs arrange themselves in a particular order (often pictured as a pyramid) and that once certain basic needs are satisfied other higher ones are tended to.

The most intrinsic human needs (the base of the pyramid) are for survival requirements such as food, clothing and shelter. Until we have these things, most of our energy will naturally be consumed with attaining them. Once these needs are met, however, we tend to pursue — in ascending order — needs for safety and security (so that our means of living will not be snatched away), social needs (so that we may relate to and be accepted by others), esteem needs (so that we may evaluate ourselves highly and earn the respect of others), and self-actualization needs (so that we may achieve our greatest potential).

The hierarchy-of-needs theory provides us with a way of understanding and explaining various aspects of human behavior. One tenet that has been extrapolated from it is that the actions of individuals — and by extension the driving forces of societies — are determined by what is perceived as the strongest need. For example, as our standards of living have increased (meeting physiological and security needs), Americans have tended to focus more energy on things like continuing education (meeting esteem and actualization needs).

It's about time

Now, however, let us consider a need which Maslow did not name as a distinct category, but which virtually all trend-watchers agree is emerging as the predominant one of the 21st century: the need for time. Poll just about any group of workers (and believe us, we have) and you will find that their chief complaint is that they do not have enough of it; that they desperately want more of it; that they are willing to make tradeoffs for it. These workers will be the "new best friend" of any employer that helps them put more time back where it belongs, i.e. in their personal lives instead of at the office.

Why did Maslow leave the need for time out of his hierarchy? Although he did not specifically enumerate it, we believe that time is an implicit, integral element of <u>all</u> the higher human needs — so obvious and fundamental that it goes without saying. Try having in-depth relationships without adequate time to nurture those relationships. Try pursuing meaningful and satisfying interests outside your job (hobbies, travel, education, volunteer work) without sufficient time to put enough into them or get enough out of them.

The problem is that too many of us have tried fulfilling these kinds of needs on the fly — depriving our families and friends of our presence, and cheating ourselves of the non-monetary riches life has to offer. We all know the stretched-thin anxiety, the restlessness and the "quiet desperation" that can result. Without time to pursue higher needs, we are effectively stuck in the bottom half of Maslow's pyramid. That's an unrewarding place to be.

In a kind of collective epiphany, members of today's workforce have come to realize the intrinsic value of the precious hours that comprise our lives. Time is no longer considered the luxury it may have been in former eras; rather, it's a requisite commodity.

This trend is spreading widely, accelerating quickly, and is here to stay — for once a need is recognized as such, the desire for meeting it is unlikely to be suppressed. To quote a *Wall Street Journal* millennial prediction, with which we wholeheartedly agree, "The value workers place on time vs. money will continue to shift in favor of time." [1]

Who is it, exactly, that needs and values time as never before? Virtually all of us. The "time value" cuts across generations and genders. It is demographically democratic. We all feel we need it, albeit for various reasons. It stands to reason that since a need impacts behavior, this powerful feeling of need is altering the way we do and do not wish to work.

Increasingly, studies point out that the top priority of employees is having control over their time via job flexibility. [2] By looking at who these employees are, and why they want this latitude on the job, we will see how their prioritization points the way, inevitably, toward the end of work as we know it.

The graying Boomers

We'll begin our demographic tour with the aging Baby Boomers. We're not starting here because this is the group to which we ourselves belong (we confess, at least, to the "Boomer" part). We do so because, by virtue of its sheer massive numbers, this group has had a deeply significant effect on society as a whole and will continue to do so for decades to come.

Why does the Baby Boom generation increasingly value time? There are numerous reasons. First, many have already achieved a degree of financial security, meeting the base-of-the-pyramid needs. Second, the reality of aging makes individuals acutely aware of mortality and its natural time limitations.

As the eternally valid law of supply and demand tells us, people value that which is in limited supply. Realizing on a gut level what they have always known intellectually — though pretty much ignored — Americans entering middle age are suddenly keenly aware that if they don't change their priorities, they may not have time to do all the things they have long yearned to do: scale a mountain peak, improve their golf game, write a novel, take up Zen, or volunteer in their communities.

Then, of course, there are the relationships to which Boomers want to devote more time. They want to spend quality hours with their growing children and, increasingly, with grandchildren. Moreover, many in this "sandwich generation" will want to — and in some cases be obliged to — allot a substantial amount of time to caring for their own aging parents. Indeed, eldercare issues are among the most significant reasons for Boomers to rearrange their work schedules, even though they may not always cite this reason to their employers. 3

So Boomers want time, but they also want to keep on doing fulfilling work. For this relentlessly active generation, it is unlikely that upper-pyramid needs for self-esteem and self-actualization will ever be perceived as completely divorced from meaningful work. Graying Boomers will want to keep working — even when chronologically of "retirement age" — in order to feel useful, stay up-to-date, and keep their lives optimally interesting and challenging. Besides, with life spans on the increase, they will not want to (and in some cases, will be unable to) rely completely on their investment income and Social Security to maintain the lifestyles to which they have become accustomed.

We ought not be surprised, then, at an AARP poll that tells us 80 percent of Boomers say they will continue to work — at least part-time — in their so-called retirement years. 4 (Even as we write this, 40 percent of AARP's members are still working.) Similar surveys — such as one conducted by Civic Ventures, a nonprofit organization in California, show like results, prompting Mark Freedman, the president of that organization, to comment, "the golden years are dead." 5

In fact, those years will be richer than ever — but also distinctively different than ever before. For the duration of their lives, it is clear that graying Boomers will remain in the workforce. ("You'll have to carry us out!" a peppy 70-something consultant told us recently.) They will carve new niches and bend all the rules, but they will remain a powerful presence.

So what do employers think of all this? The savvy ones are thrilled. The less-savvy ones will be thrilled, too, once they realize this is going to save them a tremendous amount of pain. Indeed, this demographic development is a highly fortuitous one for the business world. Were it not for the Boomers' tenacity as workers, American companies would be faced with a monumental and devastating loss of valuable human resources.

Just imagine the loss of collective experience and expertise (the "brain drain," as some have called it) that would set organizations reeling were the over-50 set to depart the workforce en masse. A work world without grownups! Ultimately, all that ponder this scenario agree it presents anything but a pretty picture.

Remember our favorite adage: People change when the pain of changing is less than the pain of not changing. With such imminent pain on the horizon, things will have to change with regard to the "rules" of work for graying Boomers. The implicit workplace bargain in the offing: Boomers will stick around — and cheerfully. Employers, for their part, will provide nothing less than a radical restructuring of jobs.

Graying Boomers will segue from full-time to part-time work in a gradual transition that may take place over years. Their part-time work may consist of doing the same thing they did before, but less of it; or it may veer more toward consulting, or toward a mentor track in which they counsel, coach and instruct the up-and-coming. Eventually, the senior workforce may alternate periods of work with extended downtime devoted to travel, eldercare or other endeavors. Whatever agreements graying Boomers reach with their employers, one thing is certain: They will irrevocably change the work culture.

Generation X

Of course, whither go the Boomers, Generation X follows — albeit in their own inimitable fashion, and at a different pace.

Generation X (the appellation for those born between 1965 and the late 1970s) also feels strongly about flexible work arrangements. But unlike the Boomers, they are unwilling to wait for them. While Boomers, in their younger years, were conditioned to think "having it all" meant single-mindedly pursuing their careers while twisting themselves into pretzels trying to tend to life's other areas, Generation X watched from the wings and didn't like what it saw.

Eschewing workaholism — not because they're "slackers" but because they hold a "whole life" view of success — many Gen-Xers believe a flexible job is the only job worth having. They are hardly shy about asking for concessions from employers with regard to flexibility, and will quit and find another job (or opt for the free-agent route) if they don't get them.

Our research shows that women in the 25-35 age group are three-and-a-half times more likely than are women of the Boomer generation to quit to obtain a flexible or part-time position, even before having children. And 72 percent of women under 35 are likely to propose a flexible work arrangement to their current employers, compared with 30 percent of female Boomers. Our research also shows that all Gen-Xers — men and women combined — are three times as likely to quit a job due to lack of flexibility than are their Boomer counterparts.

Another interesting statistic: Gen-Xers are only half as likely as Boomers to fear that their careers will suffer if they choose to work in a flexible capacity. These folks, to put it mildly, are a confident bunch. They believe that alternative work arrangements are not so much a privilege as a right. Whether or not you applaud their attitude (and we do), companies that want to mine the skills and potential of these talented, educated individuals are already acquiescing. In the future, many more will do the same

— making this the first generation able to live out the bulk of its work life in the new work mode.

Generation Y

Now let's look at one more generation. Generation Y has commonly come to refer to the children who were born from the late 1970s to the mid-1990s. These are the Boomers' babies. One of their key distinguishing features is their level of comfort with the world of clicks, bits and bytes. Indeed, members of this group have been exposed to the myriad wonders of technology from the time baby monitors were perched beside their cribs — and most of them had pre-school computer CD-ROMs displayed in front of them as soon as they could sit up.

Of course, with regard to this generation, the phrase "wonders of technology" is a misnomer. "What wonders?" this Net-surfing, pager-carrying, Game Boy-toting, Napster-downloading crew would ask. They take it all for granted. They accept as gospel the Moore's Law view of the universe, which basically tells us that the rate at which technology moves forward is only going to get faster, then faster still.

Let's face it. No way is Generation Y going to sit in a cubicle all day long to earn a living. They live an existence in which the promises of tomorrow's technology are not some vague World's Fair Futurama, but imminent realities. They have not only seen the future; they are the future. They will work where, when and how they choose — quite simply, because they can.

Highly creative and entrepreneurial (traits prized and reinforced by their proud Boomer moms and dads), Generation Y members intrinsically understand that value comes from what is produced, regardless of how long the production took or where the work was done. With this truth firmly embedded in their minds, and with their brains literally wired from birth for technological wizardry, they will find workplace opportunities their elders never imagined. By the year 2010, companies that don't go along will miss out on the best and the brightest of this generation. If you think this sounds like a formula for disaster, you are right.

Working mothers

So now we are in a situation where various groups of people, for various reasons, are coming to expect and insist on flexible work options. But let's take a moment and look at where it all began. Working mothers played — and will continue to play — a huge part in the shift in the work culture.

The two of us, successful former ad executives, were effectively "benched" after the birth of our first children. We would sit at the local park each day and watch as the most astonishing parade of accomplished and talented women — accountants, attorneys, marketing directors, and the like — patrolled the sandbox. For the first time in history, children were routinely being born to women like us — older, that is, and with established careers. Happy as we all were to be available for our children, many of us were feeling deprived of those upper-pyramid needs that are tied into doing our jobs well and being respected as professionals. Many of us also felt economic pressures as inflation and the costs of modern child-drearing (larger homes, college funds, extracurricular activities galore) ratcheted up the costs of having a family in the first place.

The dilemma: What to do with ourselves — and how to do it in such a way that no one and nothing else suffered too badly?

It was a conundrum that we in this group would struggle with for the rest of our working lives. Those who thought we had finally figured out our balancing acts realized that even flexible jobs had to be more flexible. As we had more children — and the ones we already had grew old enough to need us at parent-teacher conferences, visits to the pediatrician, and school trips to the aquarium ("the teacher asked why you haven't had a turn on the bus yet, Mom") — this became even more apparent.

Younger women, having learned from our experience, are not so much following in our footsteps as scouting out easier pathways from a better vantagepoint. At a much earlier stage in life they are taking a more realistic view of what parenthood entails and how exacting a job it is in its own right, and they are thinking and planning ahead.

Today's younger mothers know up front what we mostly discovered as we muddled along. That is, once women become mothers they face a decades-long commitment that remains high in intensity, although it varies extensively with regard to its day-to-day duties. Consequently these women are far more assertive than their elders were in dealing with employers or prospective employers. They want jobs that can bend with them. They will get them, too. Employers will increasingly recognize the value of those who have amassed so much life wisdom so early in the game, and will increasingly understand that someone who can manage her children can manage anything — including her time and her responsibilities — with aplomb.

Working dads

Until recently, 85 percent of the job applicants in our files who were seeking non-traditional employment options were women. We are now starting to see some shift, as more and more men seek the same. In the very near future we anticipate that between a third and half of those individuals seeking flexible job opportunities will be men. Among the many reasons for this is the rise of a new American social phenomenon: the working dad.

What do we mean, "working dad"? Dads have always worked, of course. But the "work" part was their emphasis, their raison d'être. When we were children, both men and women saw a father's role as primary breadwinner of the household. Of course, it was great when Dad would spend time horsing around with us kids or take us places without Mom along, or just let us hang around while, say, he puttered in the garage. But these things were special treats, as opposed to the norm. In our generation, no matter how much our fathers loved us, we all lived with the fact that their time with us was limited.

Today's fathers — perhaps because they felt the lack of their own dads so keenly — want to be different. Some are aging Boomers, having a last go at fatherhood by adding a young child to their family, and determined to be both emotionally and physically present for their kids this time around. But most are Gen-Xers who, from the get-go of their families' inceptions, are laying waste to the classic male stereotype. A recent national poll found that more than four-fifths of men aged 20-39 said having a work schedule that allowed them more time with their family took precedence over earning a higher salary or having a more challenging or prestigious job. [6]

Interestingly, this prompted Paula Rayman, director of the Radcliffe Public Policy Center, which commissioned the study, to state: "Young men are beginning to replicate women's sensibilities instead of women in the workplace trying to be more like men." [7] And therein lies a potential problem; namely, perception.

Men who wish to prioritize family time can face on-the-job challenges particular to their gender. In a work culture imbued with a lot of yang values (never complain, never let the team down no matter what it costs you personally), some employers — even those who give lip service to being family friendly — may view a man's desire to be more of a presence on the home front as a bit too yin for their taste. For example, despite the fact that, under the federal Family and Medical Leave Act, men as well as women have a right to take personal time off from work, many men have experienced pressure not to do so. (Some also fear that if they do it will be perceived as "unmanly.")

The good news is that men who are sticking to their guns and insisting on some form of alternative work arrangement often find that the initial resistance of employers recedes and their career prospects actually improve. Skeptical bosses watch working dads do what working mothers did before them — intelligently balance commitments, maximize work time with greater efficiency, plan more effectively, and remain more focused — and their opinions alter. They also observe that working dads are better able to help those whom <u>they</u> manage handle work/life conflicts with less stress and fewer negative consequences.

Further good news has simply — but powerfully — to do once again with sheer numbers. Despite ingrained prejudices in the work culture, more and more fathers are tapping into family-leave benefits, opting for teleconferences over out-of-town business trips, and insisting on flexible work options that will have them home for dinner more than just a few times a week. More than any legislation or official company policy, the strength of these numbers is what will make itself felt. For each and every dad who opts for flexibility, hundreds more will follow. It is our expectation that ultimately all employers will honor the concept of "working parent," be that parent male or female.

The people track = the profit track

Thus far we have spent a lot of time documenting how needs and numbers will compel employers to give workers the flexibility they want. But we don't want to give the impression that this is a one-sided equation, with all benefits accruing to employees and none to the organizations that employ them. In fact, nothing could be further from the truth.

If employers were merely capitulating to employee demands, with no payoff for themselves, we would not be predicting so major a shift in the work culture. Indeed, were not the enlightened self-interest of employers such a large factor in this whole phenomenon, they would likely rescind the "perk" of flexibility once the labor market expanded and the economy slowed down. But that is not going to happen.

Organizations are going to co-create and adapt to the New Workplace along with their employees. They will do this not just to avoid pain but because once they make these changes they will flourish as never before. The workplace revolution will have become workplace evolution — its initially remarkable changes becoming as entrenched as, say, the changes that got mankind up and walking on two legs and using the opposable thumb.

Just how will companies realize their bottom-line gains with regard to flexible work options? Let us count the ways…

The commitment factor (because money can't buy you love)

While in the midst of writing this chapter, one of us had to dash over to a local McDonald's to retrieve a child from a birthday party. There on the counter beside the cash registers was a stack of yellow flyers with bright red lettering. "Moms, Dads," it said, "looking for part-time work when the kids are in school?" And then: "Students…looking for spending money during the school year?" The flyer went on to detail a flexible work schedule for parents (9 a.m. to 2 p.m., holidays and summers off) and youngsters (weekend hours and early evening hours from 4 p.m. to 8 p.m.). How wise on McDonald's part and how indicative of what's in it for a company that provides job flexibility: Help employees get their needs met, and they will meet yours.

In today's competitive environment, it is extremely difficult to attract and retain high-caliber employees, not just in typical high-turnover enterprises such as fast food but virtually throughout the business world. Like it or not, gone are the days when an individual will stay with a company out of a sense of duty, or because they are waiting for that extra week's vacation at the end of 10 years, or because they already know where the coffee machine is located. Defection in the ranks is commonplace. In fact, employee turnover was nearing a 20-year high as we neared the end of 2001.

In many industries, the standard statistic is that it can cost as much as one-and-a-half times an employee's yearly salary to replace that employee. This amount factors in such items as recruiting, training and hiring. But let's talk about what is not factored in: intellectual capital and special skills.

What price can a company put on a sales rep who can sell ice to Eskimos, or a banker who will deliberately fudge a golf game to keep a client happy? What value should be placed on the attorney who writes top-notch briefs in record time, or the accountant who somehow manages to find a few critical dollars at the end of each quarter? How about a detail-obsessed administrator an entire department would be lost without? The truth is that people are now and will always be a company's greatest resource.

As Lester Thurow, the noted MIT economist, writes in his book, *Building Wealth: The New Rules for Individuals, Companies and Nations*: "Knowledge is the new basis for wealth. This has never before been true. In the past when capitalists talked about their wealth, they were talking about ownership of plants and equipment or natural resources. In the future when capitalists talk about their wealth, they will be talking about their control of knowledge." [8] This prediction, with which we concur wholeheartedly, explains why good employees are so valuable. From a technical standpoint, one might say that people are the ultimate database. In plain English: They know stuff. And without the stuff they know, a company is nowhere.

An organization's knowledge base cannot survive intact, let alone build on itself efficiently, without significant employee retention. That is why the very best organizations are already making retention a top priority, and why this trend will continue.

Since we already know that flexibility is the one thing most employees desire, it is — *ipso facto* — the one thing most likely to induce qualified people to take jobs and keep them. In fact, in a recent survey of 352 human resources executives by the American Management Association, flexible schedules were ranked as a more effective retention tool than stock options, pay-for-performance and bonuses. By restructuring jobs so employees can make room for other things, companies get the elusive thing that money cannot buy: loyalty of the truest, bluest variety. Furthermore, traditional retention tools like raises and bonuses have a high price tag, whereas offering flexibility costs a company nothing.

The productivity factor (because happy employees actually like to work)

Let's stay with the subject of costs for a bit. In the previous chapter, we began to discuss how flexibility lowers job stress. Decreased stress, in turn, leads to less job turnover. It also leads to lower medical costs, fewer disability claims, less employee absenteeism, and the like. But these cost-lowering benefits don't tell the whole story of how flexibility impacts finance. A flexible work environment not only results in substantial cost-savings but also in dramatic value-addition.

Contented employees who feel they have increased control of their life and time are not just healthier employees — physically and mentally — but employees who do more work and do it well. Flexibility and productivity go hand in hand.

At Flexible Resources, we conducted a side-by-side survey of 200 employees with flexible schedules and the managers at the 50 companies that employed them. In our findings, 56 percent of managers reported that employees working flexible schedules were "more productive per hour" than comparable staff working a full-time conventional schedule. The remaining 44 percent rated productivity the same, with none of the managers saying that workers on flexible schedules were less productive. Managers also found workers on flexible schedules to be more focused (50 percent), more professional (29 percent), more motivated (23 percent), and better able to meet deadlines (21 percent) than those employed full-time. None of the managers rated the flexible-schedule workers as less proficient in any of these areas.

Why are flexibly scheduled workers such solid performers? Perhaps because they approach their jobs with a distinct mindset. Knowing they have X amount of time in which to accomplish A, B and C, they quickly develop a knack for making the most of face-time and keen instincts for cutting through the usual stultifying office chit-chat. Goal-oriented, and often cheerfully apolitical, they know what's important and prioritize accordingly.

What's more, because "flexed" employees generally have ample time to attend to family matters and other personal affairs outside the office, they are less likely to be absent. (Family matters cause more job absenteeism than illness.) When on the job, they are less preoccupied with outside commitments and thus less apt to sneak around in order to tend to real-life chores.

Finally, they tend to be less stressed and better refreshed than do their traditionally scheduled colleagues (more sleep, fewer traffic nightmares!). They tend less towards burnout and have a good deal of energy. With their upper pyramid needs more fully satisfied, they feel better about themselves and hence are better equipped than they might otherwise have been to take on new challenges.

All in all, we find that "flexed" employees are...well...flexible. They are accustomed to being outside the box, and will take on new responsibilities and bring a fresh perspective. In our experience, they also tend to be relatively optimistic. Perhaps because, although on-the-job irritants don't disappear when one works in a non-traditional mode, they suddenly don't seem quite so bad compared with the big picture.

Of course, some employers remain skeptical about just how much value a "flexed" workforce will create. For them we would like to quote Ronald E. Compton, former CEO of Aetna Life and Casualty. "What would I say to a CEO who resists greater employee flexibility because of concerns about loss of accountability and productivity?" asked Mr. Compton. "I'd hope he was a competitor and I'd keep my mouth shut. Companies that don't believe in this are going to be trapped by it in the end." [9]

The techno-global factor (because 9 a.m. in New York is 9 p.m. in Jakarta)

Finally, there is another compelling reason for companies to institute, and to profit from, flexible work options. That reason has to do with the ways in which the world itself is evolving.

It's no secret that the day of the so-called global village has arrived. The vast majority of countries in the world are interconnected via market economies. Chances are that the companies most people work for have links around the world, be they to subsidiaries, suppliers, customers, or all of these. Technology enables all parties to be in touch almost instantaneously, on a 24/7 basis, regardless of where they are on the planet — and regardless of who may or may not be sitting at a desk in an office cubicle.

The development of e-business will continue at an exponential rate. It will be fueled by developments like a round-the-clock New York Stock Exchange and recently passed "e-signing" legislation that allows businesses and consumers to seal legally binding agreements with electronic signatures in lieu of handwriting. But mostly we will do more and more business anywhere, anytime, simply because we can. We will take this state of affairs for granted and never look back. All of which renders the traditional 9-to-5 work model an anachronism and an irrelevancy.

For their own success, organizations will need employee coverage that enables customers' needs to be met as they arise. That might be at noon, midnight, 5 a.m. or 9 p.m. It might be Monday, or it might be Sunday. Clearly, an excellent, inexpensive way to obtain such coverage is by flexing employees' schedules.

Flexed schedules can easily enhance an organization so that its whole becomes far greater than the sum of its parts. For example, we worked with a company that achieved this by staffing a particularly pivotal position with a job share. By hiring two professionals of similar ability and experience to work when they wanted to work, the position was staffed 12 hours a day. Imagine such an arrangement magnified, so that entire departments and entire divisions could have expanded coverage at no one's expense and to everyone's advantage.

A flexibility formula tailored to make employees happy and one tailored to make customers happy can be one and the same. Critical deadlines can be met with ease, while critical staff is content, loyal, and energized — with options available to them that make sense for their lives. Best of all, this is not a short-term strategy designed to give some a bigger piece of the pie; it is a permanent way to create a bigger pie for all to share.

❖   ❖   ❖   ❖   ❖

At this point in time, the majority of working people and employers are somewhat familiar with the concept of flexibility. But what may not be immediately clear is its enormous power. When we first started, even we were unaware of just how far it could go.

We remember our very first candidate, JoEllyn. She was a senior brand manager with an MBA who had a simple desire: She wanted to work 9 a.m. to 1 p.m. and be at home for her boys after school. We remember the corporate client with whom we made a match, a major food conglomerate that wanted a full-time associate product manager but couldn't find anyone at their budget level who could do the job. JoEllyn had the expertise to carry out the massive product launches a more junior person could not handle. She took the job, on the schedule she requested, and launched a new line of specialty yogurt with enormous success. Later, as JoEllyn's life continued to evolve, she left this position. But she was still available at a moment's notice as a consultant who knew the organization and could offer high-level help without the company having to suffer through additional hiring costs or lay-off problems.

As we watched JoEllyn and others we placed thrive, and the companies that hired them prosper, it dawned on us how satisfyingly, stupefyingly win/win this all was. It was then we realized that we were not just in the placement business. We were in the business of helping to reinvent business itself.

We trust our overview of work as we know it and work as it can be has piqued your interest. In the next two sections of the book we offer specific guidelines for maximizing the potential of flexibility, using strategies which are based on our more than 13 years of hands-on experience.

3

Right Options/Right People: Is Non-Traditional Employment for You?

There are two roads to happiness. The first is to be content with what you have; the second is to get what you want.

Are alternative work arrangements what you want? Should you be one of the tens of millions of workers that pursue them in the very near future? This chapter is meant to help you decide. If the answer is yes, we will help you get ready to create an action plan for achieving your goal.

A flexible spectrum

First, we'd like to go over the many types of employment arrangements that fall within the umbrella term of flexibility. By flexibility we mean anything outside the traditional 9-to-5, five-day-a-week arrangement, including permanent part time, telecommuting, job-sharing, short-term and long-term contract work, and even full-time positions in the virtual office. This is a broad spectrum of options, so even if you think you already know what you want, we suggest taking a close look at all of them. You may discover one you never considered before, thereby expanding your personal range of opportunity. What's more, you may want to make mental — and literal — notes about arrangements that aren't quite right for you at the moment, but which may gain appeal down the line. Happily, what the future holds for many of us is the ability to design and redesign work schedules as our needs and priorities change.

Indeed, in years to come we may see flexible arrangements and combinations that haven't been thought of yet. Having said that, the following are some of the flexible options you are most likely to find embraced today by companies open to non-traditional modes — as well as some of the benefits and a few caveats to keep in mind with regard to each.

Flextime

We've noticed that flextime (also known as flex*i*time) is sometimes used by the media as a generic term for any and all flexible work arrangements. But in corporate-speak it actually connotes an arrangement that enables employees to take advantage of workday schedules other than the usual 9-to-5. In many cases, employees are required to be present during certain "core" hours (e.g. 10 a.m. to 3 p.m.) to attend meetings, be available during peak customer contact times, and so on.

Flextime generally requires a five-day 40-hour week, and was the very first — and as such a fairly conservative — divergence from the traditional work schedule. The idea originated in the late 1960s in Germany (to relieve traffic congestion) and Switzerland (to attract mothers to the workforce). In the United States, Hewlett-Packard was the policy's first adherent because the company believed it would be a low-cost way to keep employees happy. [1]

Hewlett-Packard was proved right, and flextime caught on with other companies that quickly discovered the policy did more than goose their employee morale. It allowed them to extend their coverage and service hours, which in turn helped increase efficiency, productivity and customer satisfaction. It also cut down on overtime costs and substantially reduced employee tardiness and absenteeism.

From an employee's point of view, what could be wrong with flextime? For those with no objection to a five-day week as long as its hours are staggered, not much. But if you are seriously considering asking an employer to grant you this option, there are a few things to think about.

Caveat — If truly flexible flextime is what you're after, you may need to help an employer think outside the box. What we mean is that, in most cases, flextime employees simply sign up for early starting and ending times, as opposed to exploring what else might be available. A straight 7 a.m. to 3:30 p.m. schedule is far more common than one that's 10 a.m. to 8:30 p.m., or a schedule that runs on the early track three days a week and on the late track the other two. However, a late-starting, late-ending schedule might be a more practical choice for someone who is simply not a morning person or who wants to be home in the early morning to get the kids organized and off to school. Likewise, a schedule that runs on one track on Mondays, Wednesdays and Fridays, but on a second track on Tuesdays and Thursdays, might be just the thing for someone juggling numerous outside-the-office commitments.

There is little sense in being a sheep and choosing the most popular flexible option because you think it will be the least controversial. We suggest investigating the practical consequences of any schedule you aim to ask for up front. What you find may surprise you. For instance, we know someone who moved to Los Angeles, took a new job, and opted for an early flextime schedule to avoid traffic. Alas, she was struck by how vastly crowded her particular freeway route was between the hours of 5:30 and 7:30 a.m. (The explanation she was given was that Californians who work in financial markets go in early to match their work hours with their Wall Street counterparts). Since she discovered she made significantly better driving time if she waited until between 9 and 10 a.m. before heading into the office, she asked to have her schedule altered accordingly.

Caveat — We suggest that once you begin flextime you assume an attitude of responsibility for monitoring your own hours. On the arrival end, things will obviously go better if you keep your commitment as closely as possible. (Remember that employers see reduced tardiness as a key benefit of the policy.) But this is less of a potential problem for employees — who, after all, should be able to keep to an arrival time that suits them specifically — than the end-of-the-day challenge.

The end-of-the-day challenge can take a number of forms. In some instances, early-start employees may find it hard it tear themselves away even after eight full hours on the job if their colleagues (who, albeit, came in later) are still toiling. They fear it doesn't look right, and may be reluctant to leave. In truth, some managers tend to forget — especially at the beginning of an alternative arrangement — that flextime employees who started at 7 a.m. have already put in a full day by 3 p.m. As for late-start employees charged with the task of closing up shop, it can be difficult for any conscientious person to simply turn out the lights and turn on the voicemail system if there still seems to be more to do. And, of course, there is always more to do. But as Scarlet O'Hara famously noted, "Tomorrow is another day."

We're not suggesting that working on flextime ought to turn you into a relentless clock-watcher who won't hang around a nanosecond over your agreed-upon hours. But be prepared to assert your prerogatives when necessary. It will help others acclimate to your schedule, and will become less necessary as time goes on.

The compressed workweek

The compressed workweek option allows employees the opportunity to squeeze what is usually still a 40-hour workweek into fewer than five days. Often the resulting configuration is four workdays of 10 hours each (e.g. 7:30 or 8 a.m. to 5:30 or 6 p.m.).

This alternative originated in the 1970s, when a major gasoline shortage put a kink in traditional commuting habits. But it rapidly caught on with manufacturers that wanted to keep plants open seven days a week while affording their employees greater choice. It also became popular in other industries that required seven-day-a-week coverage, such as health-care, recreation, and small public agencies like police and fire departments.

If you don't work in one of these situations, you may not have thought about a compressed workweek. However, it does offer a number of pluses for employees, including a weekday off for tackling errands otherwise impossible to fit in. It generally makes commuting easier, too, by circumventing peak rush hours. We also know of situations where parents have used compressed workweeks to their particular advantage. For example, if Mom works 40 hours Monday through Thursday and Dad works 40 hours Tuesday through Friday, there are only three midweek days when they need to arrange daycare for their three children.

Caveat — If there is one thing we would caution with regard to the compressed workweek, it's the fatigue factor. Ten-hour days are long ones — especially if there's a lengthy drive at each end. But if you don't think your job performance will suffer, or that you'll doze off at the wheel en route home (and need to spend your extra day off recuperating on the sofa), this might be the option for you.

Permanent part time

Permanent part time is one of the most dynamic and far-reaching flexible options available in the workplace today, and its growing acceptance is a major leap forward. Permanent part time — by which we mean any steady arrangement in which an employee works fewer than 35 or 40 hours a week — is ideally suited to the way we work now and will work in the future. This is where flexibility takes wing.

Part-time work is a wonderful flexible option for many employers and employees alike. But when professionals think about working part-time, they are concerned that doing so may inflict a stigma upon them. They fear they may be denied advancement because employers won't take them seriously. Employers, for their part, have been known to worry that a part-time professional will not be able to get the job done. (False, as we'll soon show.)

Changing workforce demographics and our transition to first a service-based and then an information-based economy are combining to create a greater variety of such positions than ever before. Meanwhile, initial fears seem to be on the wane.

Today, permanent part-time jobs are an important aspect of a transitional strategy as employees change fields of employment, go back to school for further training, or cut back on work hours to focus more on family life and other pursuits. For many in the workforce, a permanent part-time job also holds long-term appeal as an optimum work/life solution.

Employers, too, are recognizing the benefits of hiring qualified, experienced and dedicated personnel for part-time positions. In many instances, we have witnessed the benefits of a part-time solution firsthand.

For instance, a large number of our part-time placements were made after employers had already conducted exhaustive searches for qualified full-timers at particular salary levels and had come up empty-handed. At that point — necessity being the proverbial mother of invention — they were willing to consider another kind of solution: what we call strategic staffing. Instead of defining the type of candidate they needed by the price they wanted to pay, they let us fill the bill with people who had the right skills and experience but would not be spending 40 hours a week in the office. (Our mantra to employers is "focus on results, not face-time.") These companies thus succeeded in attracting candidates who happily accepted the salary level offered in exchange for a permanent part-time schedule and the ability to pursue a career that didn't place an undue burden on their family life.

What happens then? Basically, employers notice that the work that needs to get done is, in fact, getting done, despite a diminishment in face-time. Take the candidate we placed in a 30-hour-a-week position as a human resources benefits administrator. She actually replaced a full-timer who had been idle much of the day. It didn't take long before her employer noticed that this part-timer generated higher output levels than the full-timer ever did.

Until now, companies have often resisted this path unless they were forced to traverse it. But we believe we are approaching a kind of critical mass, in which the good reputation of part-time employees will help create a new mindset. Recruiters will come to embrace a reality that has been under their noses for quite some time, and they will save a great deal of effort by opening more positions to part-timers from the start.

Caveat — Although the workplace will come to value part-timers more and more, our greatest caveat is that part-time workers need to value themselves. For all the positives of part-time permanent employment, we have noticed that candidates who accept such positions often have lingering reservations. The 30 hour-a-week benefits administrator we mentioned was pleased with her schedule, since it allowed her to be available to her teenage daughter during after-school hours (when teens are most likely to get into trouble). Still, she worried whether she would henceforth be branded a "second-class citizen" in the work environment. She was particularly concerned about the issue of re-entry. After all, someday she might decide to work on a full-time basis again (perhaps when an empty nest replaced a full house). Would she command the full-time salary she merited after daring to pare back on her work hours for a period of time? The answer was yes, we told her, as long as she believed she deserved it.

If you choose part-time employment, there is absolutely, positively and emphatically no need to hang your head. You are clearly a person who knows what you want and has the fortitude to make it happen. You are a person who can organize your life so your priorities are met, and that is no small feat. Do not neglect to value and tout these qualities in yourself, and potential employers will value you as well.

Job-sharing

We believe that job-sharing is one of the most exciting options around. Ideally suited for the global economy and the 24/7 workplace, it is the only flexible option that offers employers full-time coverage, and then some.

In a job share, two employees share responsibility for one job. The most common arrangement is when each employee works three days a week, including one day of overlap with their counterpart (with salary and benefits prorated). We recently brokered such an arrangement for a large insurance company that was faced with losing the financial professional who directed one of its securities accounting departments. When that employee announced she wanted to go part time, the company was unable to find a candidate who possessed both the people and technical skills the job required. We provided an ideal job-share partner with similar skills and experience. This is known as an <u>equal skill-set job share</u>. It works very well, but there are also variations on its theme.

For example, at Flexible Resources we have developed several new sets of job-share partnerships. We call the first the <u>complementary skill-set job share</u>. It consists of a two-person team, each of whom offers skills and experience in certain areas where the other partner is weak — yet together they meet every expectation and fill all the roles of the position, creating a complete package. Consider the situation where one person loves details and number crunching but hates speaking in public; meanwhile, their partner is wonderful at big-picture thinking and loves an audience. What employer would not appreciate this dynamic duo respectively preparing and giving new business presentations?

Another successful job share we developed is the <u>mentor-subordinate share</u>. In this arrangement, the team consists of a superior and a subordinate, each of whom handles the tasks to which their skills and experience are suited. The superior, no longer bogged down by lower-level tasks, is free to manage and strategize. The subordinate, meanwhile, is being mentored to take over the position when the superior is promoted. This is a highly cost-effective job share for an employer because team members are paid according to their level of responsibility. Another benefit is that the company can promote from within, giving employees the incentive to stay on.

Recently, we have also created a number of geographic job shares, in which responsibilities for a position are divided between colleagues in two separate time zones. Geographic job shares may even be shared between counterparts in two countries.

In 1985 a survey conducted for the American Management Association reported that 11 percent of responding employers were using job-sharing. [2] In the summer of 2000, a survey of over 600 human resources professionals by the Society for Human Resource Management showed that 22 percent of the companies studied offered job-sharing. [3] This is a step in the right direction, but only an initial step. However, we are certain that job-sharing will grow at an exponential rate during the remainder of this decade, because it offers so many advantages.

By offering job shares, employers can attract and retain top talent (even in a tight labor market) who want to work part time while still taking on the kinds of jobs suited to full-time responsibilities. They can gain access to two sets of ideas and experiences that play off and inspire one another. They can also be more fully in sync with workplace realities, since job-share teams are ideal solutions for the virtual workplace (where face-time is irrelevant) and in a workplace that operates 24/7.

As for employees, those we have placed in job shares report a high degree of job satisfaction. They bring greater energy to their jobs, they say, and are enthused each time they come to work, because they are not worn-out from the daily grind. In addition, they contend that it is wonderful to share mental stimulation and emotional commiseration with a job partner. For who — other than perhaps a spouse — can ultimately understand one as well as a job-share partner can?

Caveat — Job-sharing is not unlike a marriage. It is the teamwork ideal, wherein two halves create a whole that is greater than the sum of its parts. But, also as in a marriage, communication and cooperation are key. If you are an employee looking to create or find a job share, be aware of what you bring to the team and what your partner can bring. Be sure to forge a clear understanding of which partner is responsible for what, and when. Remember that "share" is the name of the game. In a successful job share, one never hoards information, contacts, or anything else. Moreover, if you tend to be the sort of person who believes "if you want something done right, do it yourself," think again before selecting this option.

Contingent employment

This is a catchall phrase referring to temporary workers, as well as consultants and contractors, who come into an organization to handle special projects. Contingent employees are not regular employees *per se*, in the sense that it is understood they will only be on board for a limited amount of time. We mention them here because we are making these placements with greater and greater frequency. In fact, on any given day there are approximately three million temporary workers on the job in this country. [4]

Contingent placements often suit the needs of our candidates, many of whom like to keep their options open as their futures unfold. In the rapidly evolving workplace, these placements also suit the needs of our clients, who appreciate such candidates for their ability to plug-and-play, i.e. instantly tackle multi-faceted tasks with alacrity.

Another reason for mentioning contingent positions is because they often transform into permalance jobs with flexible features. Many of the companies that work through us to hire professionals for short-term assignments — from high profile dot-coms to established corporate giants — have kept our candidates on the job well beyond the initial work arrangement.

Often the need for a contingent employee arises because a company's internal hiring process is so cumbersome and time-consuming that someone is actually needed to do the job while the search process goes on. The company then places a qualified candidate on a temporary basis, and because there is no long-term investment or commitment involved, tends to be accommodating when it comes to that candidate's flexible scheduling preferences. In effect, they are trying flexible arrangements on for size, and once again opting to value output over face-time.

A flexible employee can be invaluable in helping them deal with the day-to-day ins and outs of their business. Regardless of fluctuating workload or departmental dynamics, that person is there, plugging away. And because the arrangement is so economical for the company, there is no bottom-line pressure to eliminate the job. It's no surprise to us, therefore, that over 50 percent of the candidates we have placed in 90-day contingent positions stay on for more than a year. If the need that a company hired a contingent employee to fill doesn't go away neither does the employee. And if the original need should go away, the employee may find his services needed elsewhere in the organization. On the other hand, if a contingent employee wants to move on, he is not bound by a "five more years until I'm vested" mentality to stick around.

Not everyone feels this confident about the "temp" trend — as you will glean from the caveat that follows — yet we are certain that contingent employment will grow astronomically. Moreover, we are not alone in this conviction. Tom Peters, the renowned work-trends guru, predicts that in the near future freelance contractors will be more the rule than the exception, and that many projects will be performed by temporary networks that disband when their tasks are complete. [5] Margaret Regan, who has studied the workforce for consulting group Towers Perrin, concurs, predicting that less than one-third of Generation Y members ("millennials," as she terms them) will opt for steady staff jobs. Most will sign on for specific projects, she says, then take downtime upon completion to pursue other things before re-enlisting in the workforce. [6] Once again, sheer demographics are likely to spur this bandwagon onward.

Caveat — In many cases, as we've mentioned, short-term freelance arrangements often evolve into long-term permalance arrangements. In most instances, this suits all parties just fine. The companies feel they are inured against financial turndowns. The "lancers" have their much-valued freedom, and indeed sometimes make more in terms of monetary compensation than their full-time counterparts.

We are aware, however, that in some instances contingent employees may decide they would rather have their positions on an official permanent basis, often because they want the security — and the health insurance, retirement plans, and other perks and benefits — that go along with permanent hiring.

Sometimes companies are resistant to making this happen, and there are simply no guarantees that it will happen. (No, not even if you and other freelance colleagues band together and litigate, as has happened on occasion.) On the bright side, the skills and knowledge acquired in a contingent job should serve to make you more marketable than ever before and very attractive to employers in general.

Phased or partial retirement

Phased retirement, in which one gradually cuts back on work hours, and partial retirement, which essentially equates to a permanent part-time position, are options that many graying Boomers are — or soon will be — choosing. They may continue their pre-retirement roles during phased or partial retirement, or they may take on more of a consulting and/or mentoring role, transferring valuable knowledge to those who will ultimately succeed them.

We've already mentioned how such arrangements are beneficial to companies that need to prevent the "brain drain" that would occur should senior staffers exit en masse. Interestingly, as we were preparing to write this chapter we came across a *Wall Street Journal* article that really brought the point home. Entitled "Los Alamos Lab Tries to Stem the Decline of Bomb

Know-How," it began: "When John Richter retired from Los Alamos National Laboratory three years ago, he took with him nearly the equivalent of China's entire experience with nuclear weapons. China at that point had built and tested 45 warheads. Dr. Richter, one of the lab's preeminent Cold Warriors, could claim 42." [7]

The article went on to detail, somewhat alarmingly, the severe toll that the loss of older workers has taken on national defense. The solution, it said, was to pass vital accumulated expertise onto the next generation entering the weaponry field — something the Los Alamos Lab is doing by tapping "old blood" and instituting new education concerning America's nuclear arsenal, which itself is aging. If ever a scenario were tailor-made to illustrate the dangers of letting aging talent leave without sufficient overlap with younger employees, this would seem to be it. Not every situation is so evidently life-and-death but, figuratively speaking at least, the viability of any company could easily hang in the balance unless phased and partial retirement become the norm. And so they will.

Of course, phased and partial retirement also meet the needs of those approaching traditional "retirement age" who still want to participate in the workplace for all sorts of reasons — be they financial, intellectual or emotional. With people living longer, healthier and more active lives, the idea of spending 20 or 30 years ambling around the golf course or schmoozing with grandchildren lacks universal appeal. Toss some on-the-job action into the mix — especially in an environment where one's talent and experience are held in high esteem — and it begins to seem far more stimulating.

Caveat — The idea of phased and partial retirement is so sensible and so obvious we could hardly think of a caveat to add. But then we interviewed some younger workers who asked us to include their advice. As one put it: "We do value the knowledge that senior employees have to impart, as long as they are really willing to impart it. Sometimes it seems they are a little reluctant to let go, like they will be shown the door if they actually let us know all the details." So a word to the wisest: Mentoring well is one of the most productive things you can do. If your company is smart, they will reward you for that skill, not punish you. If your company isn't smart, why do you still want to hang around?

Telecommuting

Becoming ever more popular, telecommuting is an option that refers to employees who, for all or some of their work-dedicated hours, work from home or from a satellite office. Telecommuting used to be alternately referred to as flexiplace, but as technology-enabled links to the home office became increasingly widespread, the terminology shifted accordingly.

When telecommuting first gained popularity, it was most commonly found in industries whose employees were naturally far-flung. Sales and insurance reps who might live hundreds of thousands of miles from corporate headquarters would set up an in-home office, or perhaps spend some time at regional field offices, so they could keep in touch, be readily reachable at certain pre-designated hours, and remain very much part of the loop. Today, employees in many industries — particularly ones that are service-based and knowledge-based — also telecommute.

Telecommuting offers many advantages for companies that wish to save on the cost of office space, foster efficiency, and draw on a talent pool that might otherwise be unavailable to them. For employees, telecommuting is a highly popular option. Indeed, many telecommuters we know are almost evangelical about it, referring to it as "a blessing" or "a godsend." Why the near-religious fervor? Think about it. For home workers, there is no actual commuting on the days of telecommuting — unless one counts a walk down the hall or out to an office over the garage. Dressing for success is hardly an issue, and neither is buying lunch every day. For those who work in satellite offices, the commute is still far shorter than it would be otherwise, and the atmosphere at work is more casual. All this adds up to saved time, saved money and minimized stress.

Needless to say, the development of such nifty little items as the fax machine and the modem had a significant effect on the viability of telecommuting. With technological developments from high-speed Internet connections to increasingly sophisticated wireless devices careening forward, this mode of work will only become more practical. Of course, once companies realize that nearly every employee can be technologically enabled to work from home at least some of the time, it is inevitable that they will also realize many jobs don't need to be performed at the office. Indeed, some tasks are better done away from the distracting hubbub of the workplace crowd. These include writing (as we can personally attest), designing, creating computer programs, readying presentations, handling written correspondence, crunching numbers, and even returning phone calls.

And why, for example, should a customer-service call center necessarily be located in the high-overhead environment of a suburban industrial park or a city skyscraper, when satellite offices could just as easily cope with the same calls? (In a cheerier and more helpful fashion, we would bet, because employees working closer to home are generally more content.) There is, of course, no reason why. Hence the inevitability of such arrangements.

Last but certainly not least, telecommuting is ideal for the virtual company, i.e. for a company that may have a small central headquarters as a flagship but fundamentally consists of a network of the best talent from all over. To assist just such a new dot-com venture, which has a central office near Stamford, Connecticut, but many far-flung employees, we placed a project manager who basically acts as the right hand of the company president (who spends most of his time in Washington, D.C.). The manager works 30 hours a week, 30 percent of the time from home and the rest on site in the Stamford office. We also placed two attorneys with the same company, both of whom work entirely by telecommuting. These sorts of arrangements — with which all parties are thrilled, we might add — are quickly becoming a common staffing model for start-ups.

Caveat — As we will detail in a later chapter, the logistics of telecommuting need to be thought through carefully. This is not simply a matter of plopping a laptop down on the kitchen counter. Employers and telecommuting employees must work together to set commonsense standards about how work will be accomplished, when communication will take place, and so on. The ergonomics of working in an office-away-from-the-office need also be considered (no beach chairs, please).

On top of this, there is the family factor to take into account. Sometimes workers who attempt to do part of their work at home find one of their biggest challenges is getting those on the home front to cooperate. Most companies with telecommuting employees specify that such an arrangement is not a substitute for childcare, although one's children may disagree. Working at home means being at home while you work, but it also means being able to work while you're home. It's a simple enough concept in theory, but in practice it may be more complex.

Outside the box options

When it comes to work options, we like to be creative. In fact, in many instances we have arranged for "combo" employment arrangements that are outside the standard box of flexible employment. For example, an auto dealership that had dealers in three states needed a project manager with a recruiting background to set standard policies and practices for recruiting and hiring. We placed a candidate who works four days a week, but spends 65 percent of his time telecommuting and the rest at the dealerships.

Another example: When a consumer products giant was seeking a part-time promotions manager at its Westchester County, New York headquarters, they were — despite their longstanding reputation for flexible hiring — still having difficulty finding a person with the specific experience the position demanded. Because this corporation had worked with us many times over the years, they asked for access to our talent pool. It didn't take long to find just the right person, but she lived some 40 miles away. We negotiated an 8 a.m. to 3 p.m. schedule, three days at the office and one day at home. This flexible position — with which everyone was content — was a combination of part time, flextime and telecommuting. That's outside the box thinking.

Even older, more established companies see value in hiring talented professionals who will commit to a company that lets them work on a non-traditional schedule. When a certain milk product company needed to fill a marketing position, we found that the best way to staff it was with two people with different skill sets, each of whom had strengths in areas where the other was weak. Both now work two 10-hour days, providing 40 hour-a-week coverage for the company while dramatically cutting down on their own commute times. Note that this arrangement combines a compressed workweek with a job share.

As the remainder of the decade unfolds we will see — and orchestrate — other job options no one has thought of yet. And why not? As the world changes, so the workplace must change. Non-traditional options must be flexible in more ways than one. They must keep expanding and evolving to meet the requirements of new technologies, new economic realities, and new generations to come.

Right person/right job

Becoming aware of just how many flexible work options exist, and how many possibilities await, can be exhilarating. But it can also be confusing. At this point some of you may be wondering which options suit you best, and indeed whether flexible work is really the best solution for you overall.

To help you sort this out we'll look at certain traits and motivations that many of our candidates have in common. By honestly evaluating yourself — including your priorities, your practical circumstances, and your own personal skills and traits — you can see how much you have in common with them.

A demographic profile

One of the questions we are asked most often is, 'Who are the candidates seeking flexible employment? What sort of people are they?" To track trends in flexible employment, and to provide employers with a picture of the talent pool they can tap into by offering flexible work arrangements, we conducted a survey of more than 500 candidates seeking non-traditional employment through our firm's offices in four large cities. [8]

Among the things our survey analyzed were the purely demographic features of this population. We wanted to get a picture of average ages, education levels, income levels, and the like, for would-be flexible employees.

Here is some of what we discovered.

• The average age of all candidates is 39 years. Over half (53 percent) are under age 40.

• Over half of all candidates have completed some graduate-level courses. 42 percent have Master's degrees.

• 73 percent of candidates have children, although candidates aged 25 to 35 are five times more likely to be childless than are candidates aged 36 to 45.

• On average, the candidates' most recent personal income was $64,000. (However, personal income increased with the age of the candidate.)

• On average, their current combined household income was $105,000.

• Over eight in 10 (81 percent) of candidates who approach Flexible Resources are currently working or have most recently worked at the middle-management level.

What does this tell you? Basically, it explains who the "average" person seeking flexible employment is at the turn of the millennium — a snapshot moment in time. We think it will be interesting to see how closely your profile matches that of the typical candidate, since it's what an employer's human resources staff may be picturing when they think of the overall talent pool seeking flexible positions. On the other hand, don't be overly concerned if you don't match the exact picture presented. These are statistical means, and it would be rare if everyone fit them (almost as rare as having the statistical average of 2.2 children). Also, some variables are contingent upon other variables (e.g. the older one is, the higher one's income tends to be). Most important, for reasons we've detailed in the previous two chapters, we know that more people across a wide range of demographic groups are going to be drawn toward non-traditional employment options in the years ahead.

So, what if you're a 24-year-old, with $30,000 in personal income, no kids and no graduate education? What if you are 50 years old? Or never held a middle-management position? Should you even attempt to find a job with flexibility? Of course you should, if that's what seems to make sense for you. Far more critical in your decision are some of the other factors we've mentioned, such as motivation and priorities.

What's your motivation?

Why do people work at all? The answer may seem obvious. Remember Maslow's hierarchy of needs? We need to meet survival requirements before we do anything else. To survive in the modern world we need money; *ipso facto*, most people work for the money.

When we polled respondents in flexible positions who formerly worked in traditional jobs we were, therefore, not shocked when "for the money" was the reason most frequently cited for working under both circumstances. Of interest, however, is that while 49 percent of respondents said this was the most important reason for working traditionally, only 41 percent said it was the most important reason for working flexibly.

We also learned some other things of significant interest, namely:
• "Feeling good about myself" was four times as likely to be considered the most important reason for working in a flexible arrangement

compared to working a traditional schedule (36 percent and 9 percent, respectively).

• "Professional ambition" was more than five times as likely to be considered the most important reason for working a traditional schedule compared to working in a flexible arrangement (28 percent and 5 percent, respectively).

When we asked about the primary motivation for seeking flexible as opposed to traditional employment, we learned:

• The reason most frequently given for switching to a new arrangement was "work/family balance" (81 percent). The second most frequently mentioned reason was "responsibilities to my children" (65 percent).

• The next most frequently mentioned reason was "better overall quality of life."

So far we are getting a pretty clear picture of what it is that employees seeking flexible job options really value. They still want a respectable income, but they are driven more by goals of personal fulfillment and quality time with family than by corporate ladder climbing. While they still feel career growth is important ("very important" to 21 percent and "somewhat important" to another 44 percent), they realize there are numerous ways of achieving this — not all of them requiring breakneck schedules.

This prompted us to ask exactly what kind of sacrifices, if any, our respondents had made in order to obtain flexible employment. Although 34 percent said "none," 60 percent said they had sacrificed some benefits and 53 percent noted lower income. However, only 9 percent said they had settled for a less challenging position.

After all their gains and some compromises most, on balance, seemed content. When asked whether they planned to go back to full-time traditional employment sometime in the future, 40 percent said "yes," another 7 percent said "maybe," but the majority (53 percent) said "no."

Do the priorities of these flexible employees sound like your priorities? Are personal fulfillment, quality of life and work/family balance worth a possible detour from the traditional fast track? We're guessing that in many cases your answer is yes, or you wouldn't have read this far! But what about those nuts-and-bolts issues concerning money and benefits?

The average flexible employee earns $35 an hour, or an annual full-time equivalent of $73,000. (Obviously your salary will vary according to your particular profession, experience and skills). As for benefits, although we've been able to negotiate them for some of our candidates, right now fewer than one in five (19 percent) flexible employees receive full benefits as part of their compensation.

Obviously, you will need to assess your individual circumstances to see where you stand. If another working family member has a position with health insurance, a retirement plan, and so on, such a sacrifice on your part may be easier to bear. As for salary, we think you should assess not only what you are likely to make in a non-traditional arrangement in your particular field, but also something else: the actual monetary cost of working in a full-time traditional job.

According to the Bureau of Labor and Statistics, since 1982 the number of married couples in which both partners work has risen from 39 percent to 47 percent. [9] At first one may think, "Hmm, those couples must be ahead of the game." But are they?

We recently placed an attorney in a flexible three-day-a-week position at a major financial firm. Prior to this arrangement, she worked full-time and employed three separate childcare providers for her four pre-school children. Not only was she missing time with her children, but she was also spending a huge amount of her salary to do so. Does this sound like a story you've heard all too often?

Of course childcare costs are just one of the work-related expenses that add up. Even couples without children must consider the tax cost of both spouses working full-time. And everyone, married or not, needs to factor in such bottom-line costs as commuting, meals at work, work wardrobes (complete with dry cleaning), and the need to pay for things they simply don't have time to do themselves (lawn-mowing, housecleaning, etc.).

We encourage you to sit down, take a deep breath and do the math. What you find may surprise you and it will likely assist you mightily in the task of weighing potential tradeoffs.

Bringing out your best

Now we come to our final category of criteria to consider before choosing to pursue non-traditional employment. This category has to do with your own personal traits, the things that make you who you are.

People who find personal and professional happiness in the realm of flexible employment tend to have certain characteristics in common. Again, we urge you to be honest with yourself in seeing whether these traits seem to describe you. If they don't, it doesn't mean you're any less wonderful a human being. What we hope to help you determine here is simply whether or not flexible employment is likely to bring out the best in you.

Are you a self-starter? All humans desire to be part of a social group. In fact, some anthropologists and sociologists say this is the strongest human characteristic. Of course, you will still be part of a group when working flexibly. But you probably won't have the same level of reinforcement and feedback you've experienced when working in a traditional position. More than ever before, it may be your responsibility to define your job's parameters, to decide how much time to allocate to your various projects, and to communicate your progress to co-workers (with whom you may be sitting in lengthy meetings far less often).

Are you able to tolerate less socializing with co-workers? Along with less time spent talking about work with co-workers, a flexible employee will likely indulge in less of the kibbitzing that goes on around the proverbial water cooler. If this daily camaraderie is a big part of why you go to work — and, let's face it, for some people it is — then you may experience a sense of isolation should it dissipate even a little. Of course, having more time off from work will give you other social opportunities — perhaps better ones. But each individual needs to consider his or her unique situation.

<u>Are you focused and well organized?</u> If you work off site, or work on site during hours when not everyone else is around, you will have people looking over your shoulder less often. But even if you work in a virtual office, your deadlines are as real as ever. And even if you only go into an office three days a week, people still depend on you daily. They may need to contact you on days when you are not there in the flesh to obtain a particular piece of information or seek your counsel. Flexible employees must hunker down and do what needs to be done, tuning out distractions. They must keep diligent track of the status of their projects, so colleagues will never be left in the dark nor customers left out in the cold. Focus and organization are skills one can acquire and hone, but if you are not naturally inclined in this direction, a non-traditional job could prove quite challenging.

<u>Are you efficient and results-oriented?</u> Successful flexible employees are more interested in the end result of a project than in dwelling on the means to that end. Are you capable of cutting to the chase? If so, you will bring to your position the high productivity levels that employers of flexible employees have come to expect. Let your colleagues who can't tackle a task without detailing every incremental step on PowerPoint and following up with self-congratulatory memos retain their traditional schedules. They'll need the extra time.

<u>Are you apolitical?</u> Flexible employees do not have the time to spend sucking up to superiors, backstabbing supposed rivals, or contriving Machiavellian plots to replace the CEO. If you believe rewards at the workplace come from a job well done, flexibility will work for you. If you believe such rewards depend largely on crafty self-promotion, we suggest you don't even think about it. When you're not in the office, you might drive yourself crazy wondering who is plotting against <u>you</u>.

Are you a good communicator? As a flexible employee, you won't always be "just down the hall," so you will need to make certain that other people are privy to your job-related information. Hoarding such information is one of the greatest sins you can commit. To make a non-traditional option work smoothly, one needs to be vigilant about maximizing communication skills.

Are you available? You will need to be contactable by colleagues when you are not around in person. Even if you've shared every last detail of a project's status, there may be some new development for which your input is needed. In general, it's a good idea to have agreed-upon ground rules for such contact, so co-workers will know the pre-designated times when you will be calling in for messages or checking e-mails. It will be up to you to keep these commitments faithfully, and to provide emergency contact information for occasions when urgent matters arise.

By the way, these days — and forevermore — part of being available is being techno-friendly. If you hate the sound of a ringing cell phone and loathe squinting at hand-held Internet devices, working flexibly will not be your cup of latte.

Are you flexible and innovative? Right now many companies are trying on flexibility for size. That means you need to go with the flow. You and your employer may agree to try a particular schedule and work arrangement, only to find there are adjustments that need to be made to suit either or both of you. If things need to be fine-tuned, you will need to participate in that process. Or, you may need to acquire some additional skills to qualify for a particular flexible position that you know is becoming available. Or, you might be able to turn a traditionally scheduled position into a flexible one by thinking creatively about the way the job is done. The bottom line is that flexible workers must be innovative — open to new ideas, willing to think creatively, willing to take a shot. You can't expect an employer to show flexibility if you won't.

Do you know when to stop? Last, but by no means least, those with non-traditional schedules owe it to themselves to take advantage of the personal time for which they negotiated. Let's say you are supposed to work a permanent part-time 30-hour-week. Sure, stuff happens. It stands to reason there may be instances when you find yourself working a few hours more. But if you are routinely working 40 hours — either because you have a hard time stopping or because your boss or co-workers have a hard time letting you stop — well then, you are back to working a full-time schedule, and for less remuneration. So while one needs to be reasonable about extenuating circumstances, a flexibly scheduled employee must be willing to set appropriate limits and boundaries with regard to working above and beyond the call.

❖　　❖　　❖　　❖　　❖

Hopefully by now you have a better idea of whether or not flexible employment is suited to you, and vice versa. If the match seems good, you should also have an idea of which type of non-traditional arrangement may best fit your needs. The next thing you need is a plan.

This is not a time to be impulsive but instead to think things through and get thoroughly prepared. We have seen over and over again how reluctant many employees are to ask their current employers for a change from traditional to flexible arrangements. Our survey found that 64 percent of our candidates had already left their positions or were about to quit — and 59 percent said they would not even bother to ask if a flexible position could be arranged.

Why give up so easily? Our next chapter will help you to formulate a detailed written proposal that may get you exactly what you want. It will also offer some additional strategies to pursue, in the event that you don't.

PART II

Having Cake And Eating It — A Guide for Employees

"There are only a few times in organization life when [man] can wrench his destiny into his own hands..."

—William H. Whyte, Jr,
The Organization Man

4

Creating a Work Plan that Works

When we asked 500 of our job seekers if they requested a non-traditional work option from their last employer before quitting, we were astonished when 59% said no, they hadn't. When we asked why not, we began to understand. The most common reason given for not approaching their employers was they <u>believed</u> their company had a policy against it (though in many cases this turned out not to be true). The second most common reason cited was their own <u>fear of being perceived</u> as not serious about their jobs.

Look closely at these reasons and notice the pattern: Mistaken beliefs and fears of being misunderstood are what prevented employees from asking for what they wanted — what, in fact, they wanted badly enough to quit for. As for the employers involved, they never knew why skilled, productive personnel had walked out the door. They probably thought these employees were leaving for more money. Another misunderstanding!

But let's look at the other side of the coin. Of employees who do approach their current employers with proposals for job flexibility, 63 percent succeed. It's an ironic twist, to say the least. It goes to show that defeat in such situations ought not to be a foregone conclusion. Indeed, the employers who were actually given a chance to consider their employees' requests were probably delighted to have the opportunity to retain valuable, experienced talent.

We believe that the chance of defeat lessens appreciably when well constructed, thoroughly thought-out planning has taken place prior to asking an employer for flexible options. The antidotes for fear and misunderstanding are sound knowledge and effective communication. Armed with these tools, and a plan for enacting them, one can face any dragon — even employers who may genuinely not be predisposed to flexibility in the workplace.

We have nothing against spontaneity; winging it sometimes works out very well in life. Indeed, when we first started in the flexible-staffing field, we had no real plan *per se*. We had something of a vision, which grew clearer as we went along; and we had a notion — proved correct — that there would be obstacles to overcome. But now we have a great deal of experience under our belts. Moreover, we have coached and "debriefed" over a thousand employees who have successfully achieved their goals, whether by remaining with a current employer or ultimately moving on. With the benefit of cumulative hindsight, we devote this chapter to helping you make the transition from a traditional to non-traditional work arrangement smoother than it might be otherwise.

When should my plan be started?

Perhaps you're wondering if it's too early to begin planning. But we can assure you it's never too soon, even if you might not want flexibility for another six months or a year. Employers always appreciate receiving as much notice as possible with regard to your needs. Besides, if there are objections, you can use the extra time to engage in some diplomatic persuasion.

In reality, the universe does not always oblige us by giving advance notice of when there will be occurrences in our lives that require a change of habits and patterns. There is no way to know, for example, when a family member might be taken ill and require our ministrations. However, there are certain instances when we know ahead of time that we will have to change the way we work. If a new baby is going to be on the scene, for example, or if you are applying to a part-time graduate program or even considering a segue into partial retirement, early planning allows you time to mull over your options and implement a strategy.

You have nothing to lose by taking this proactive step. Even if you believe the chances of getting your current employer to cooperate are slim, we still urge you to attempt to get what you want by staying where you are. If things don't work out, you'll be a giant step ahead when it comes to negotiating with prospective employers, because you will be clear about what it is you offer and what you hope to get in return.

Put it in writing

The most important advice we can give about your plan is to <u>put what you propose in writing.</u> Putting a plan in writing helps to focus your thoughts and will also help you make your case in the clearest possible way.

Make your plan detailed. This will alleviate anxiety and negativity on the part of the person to whom you present it, and will address many of the questions they might have. Among the details to include are a description of the flexible option you would like to implement; your proposed hours of work; what responsibilities you will retain, and how the rest will be handled. Include provisions for a trial period and spell out how you believe standards of success should be applied to this arrangement.

Another critical aspect of your plan is to <u>hone in on the business perspective.</u> Don't dwell on how you'd really like some extra time with the kids. Your boss wants to know how you will make his department more productive and profitable. To this end, include any cost data you can come up with. How will your flexible position affect benefits and salary? How will it impact company revenues? If you have a sales quota, how are you going to meet it?

Obviously, you will want to <u>put the most positive spin on your proposal.</u> Stress what you have to offer, especially if your skills are unique and in demand. Avoid anything that sounds like an ultimatum or seems adversarial. To quote Abe Lincoln on the topic of persuasion:

If you would win a man to your cause, first convince him that you are his sincere friend. Therein is a drop of honey that catches his heart, which, say what you will, is the great high-road to his reason, and which, when once gained, you will find but little trouble in convincing his judgment of the justice of your cause. [1]

Also, do your homework. We recommend thorough preparation in two areas. First, check out the competition. Find out what other companies in your field are doing and how positions such as yours are handled on a flexible basis. Learning that the competition is offering innovative staffing options may help nudge your company in a similar direction. Second, price yourself so that you will be positioned to negotiate your compensation.

As a self-pricing guideline, we suggest taking your current salary and adding 30 percent. Then prorate this on a per diem basis, depending on how many days you wish to work. Why add 30 percent? To cover the costs of benefits your employer may ask you to relinquish. If you negotiate for retaining some — or all — of your benefits, you can adjust your salary accordingly. But pricing yourself ahead of time gives you a starting point from which to negotiate.

Be creative and have alternatives ready. If, for example, your position must be handled full-time, suggest a telecommuting arrangement. Alternatively, come up with a job-share partner in advance. Such forethought saves time and effort on the part of your employer. Besides, who knows better than you do with whom you'll work best?

Prepare a communications strategy. Specifically detail how you will keep in contact with the office. Note how many times a day, and at what hours, you will phone in and/or check e-mail. Let it be known how colleagues and clients can reach you when you are off site. If you already have your own communication-enabling equipment, such as a cell phone, a wireless e-mail device, and/or a home computer with a high-speed Internet connection, say so.

If a job-share proposal is what you wish to submit, we have some additional pointers. You may want to include a "two-headed resume" that spells out how you and your potential partner's strengths and talents mesh. Include how you and your partner will divide tasks, convey information to one another and to others in the department, and handle emergency situations. Last, but not least, make it clear that you and your potential job-share partner prepared this proposal together. If the two of you can get a coherent plan on paper as a team, your boss will be more likely to believe you can put that plan into action.

To whom should I give my proposal?

As for presenting your proposal, in most cases your best bet is to give it to the manager to whom you report directly. This is the person most familiar with you, your capabilities, your reliability, and perhaps even your relevant life circumstances. Moreover, this is the person who really knows, on a day-by-day basis, exactly what your job involves. Even if your company is set up in such a way that your immediate boss will have to seek approval at a higher level, his or her buy-in is critical. With your direct report manager as your greatest advocate, you stand a much better shot than you would otherwise.

On the other hand, as most of you with corporate experience know, if you start at the top you risk the prospect of interminable delays as your proposal winds its way through a Kafka-esque maze of bureaucracy. We have a friend who refers to the upper echelons of the corporate hierarchy as the "adminisphere," which he defines as the rarefied organizational layers, just above the rank and file, from which — after lengthy periods of time — irrelevant decisions tend to fall. Trust us: You don't want your proposal sitting in the adminisphere, and certainly not without a champion to push it along.

Rebutting objections means debunking myths

Naturally, not all proposals will be met with immediate, hearty approval. In fact, no matter how much solid preparation goes into them, some proposals are declined. At this point, rather than throwing in the towel, we would suggest formulating rational rebuttals to any objections that arise. Ask your employer to be specific, and respond in kind.

Since it's best to be forearmed, if possible, we will list some of the objections you're likely to encounter. Actually, over the years we have taken to calling these objections "myths we love to hate." Because that's exactly what they are — myths and misunderstandings.

We'll look at these myths one by one, offering rebuttals that may assist you in forming your own. While it makes sense to tailor your responses to your particular situation, these general points should help bolster your case for flexibility.

Myth # 1: "If I give it to one person, everyone will want it."

In our experience, this is simply untrue. Here's a notable example: One of our biggest clients, a major food-manufacturing conglomerate, fully embraces flexibility in all its forms. This company has a policy of posting all jobs, including flexible positions, internally first. Often three or four flexible jobs are posted at once. But ironically, these jobs are rarely filled internally and the company ends up repeatedly coming to us for candidates.

The truth is, although flexibility is the wave of the future, there are still many nine-to-fivers with a fear of the unknown. Upsetting the status quo is always frightening. So is making tradeoffs or concessions, no matter what the potential reward. Even when the status quo is driving us crazy, we often opt for familiar pain over unfamiliar deliverance.

But let's take this rebuttal a step further. Suppose there are some employees who, observing how well flexibility is working out for a colleague, overcome their resistance to a new paradigm and ask for a similar arrangement. This will only benefit the company in question. Our surveys of managers consistently reveal that after they have tried flexible staffing, they like it. So if, in some instances, another employee requests a flexible schedule, they may actually welcome the request. It means that yet another committed employee wants to stay, and is willing to make compromises to work things out.

Myth # 2: "Professionals who want to work part-time aren't committed."

Our studies, which are based on manager evaluations of flexible employees, prove that nothing could be further from the truth. Managers report that flexible employees are professional, productive and very committed. These employees tend to work harder and with greater focus because they have made sacrifices in order to <u>keep</u> working, and also because they have a great deal vested in making their arrangements succeed.

Managers and HR directors need to understand it is not the company that is making a sacrifice by allowing employees to work flexible schedules. The employees are the ones who willingly do so, because they recognize that the only way to restore their sanity is to bring work back into balance with the rest of their lives. To keep that balance in place, they simply need a "get the job done" attitude.

We want to emphasize that one's "level" in a company has nothing to do with whether or not a position can be handled effectively on a flexible basis. We have created flexible positions for extremely high-ranking professionals, including vice presidents and CFOs.

Myth #3: "I can't get along without full-time coverage."

The answer to this dilemma is job-sharing. As we have said, job-sharing is the only flexible option that provides employers with full job coverage, even beyond the traditional 40-hour week. Remember, job-sharing can be implemented in numerous innovative ways. In addition to two people of equal skills and experience sharing a job, it may be in a company's best interests to institute:

- A mentor-subordinate job share (in which the subordinate is groomed for promotion when the mentor moves up);

- A geographic job share (which accommodates the needs of customers in different locales and time zones);

- A complementary skill-set job share (in which two people of differing skills and experience round out a position).

Myth #4: "I can't manage someone who isn't here."

This is old thinking. A person who is doing even part of their work outside the office is under the same performance pressure as anyone else — perhaps even more, because of their enormous personal stake. What's more, the technology at our disposal makes them easily reachable. Simply because you have less face-time with them doesn't mean they have fallen off the face of the earth.

For example, we placed a woman in a telecommuting job at a major marketing firm. Equipped with a beeper and a modem, she was put to work almost exclusively outside the office. The result? The firm gave her its "Outstanding Employee of the Year Award." Most of the company didn't even realize this employee was on a flexible arrangement. The bottom line is, put the right people in the job and managing them is not a problem.

Myth # 5: "We tried it-we didn't like it."

Did they really try? What happened? Some companies make a half-hearted attempt to implement flexibility in one or two cases, but without much forethought. Perhaps they never took the time to get direct report managers on board or to disabuse those managers of any hidden prejudices equating flexible employees with second-class employees. Perhaps they never worked out an effective communication strategy between flexible employees, co-workers and subordinates.

Moreover, if you ask such employers if they ever had a problem with an employee who was on a regular schedule, they will — of course — answer yes. Did it ever occur to them to stop hiring on a regular schedule because of that? Of course not.

Myth # 6: "We already offer flexibility, sort of."

Finally, and perhaps ironically, some companies don't embrace true flexibility because they believe they already offer it. For example, every year certain publications and organizations promote lists of "family-friendly companies." If you look at these lists, you will see that most of the "innovative" things these companies are doing are hardly evidence of flexibility, family-friendliness, or anything else of much value to over-stressed employees.

Most often cited as "proof" that a company is flexible are on-site day-care, flextime (the most conservative of flexible options, which merely allows a person to shift work hours forward or backward), and dry-cleaning pick-up or similar errand-running services. But these "solutions" do nothing to get at the heart of creating a balanced life or enabling working parents to spend significantly more time with their children. In fact, some are actually devices to get people to work longer hours — at the office!

If your company responds to your proposal by showing off its own list of outdated programs, we suggest you refrain from expressing criticism or cynicism. (Remember Abe Lincoln's advice!) Instead, explain how what you want differs — and why.

What if they still say no?

Treat your flexibility request like any other negotiation. Find out where your plan falls short, and try again. Be prepared to give a little to get something back. If the answer is still no, you may need to be realistic and begin to consider other opportunities.

If you plan to look before leaping (generally not a bad idea), we suggest you look for a potential employer that actually embraces flexibility. How can you find organizations that will allow you to work in a non-traditional mode? There are numerous clues.

Search out companies that embrace new technologies. For instance, as we began writing this book, Ford Motor Company announced it would be purchasing a personal home computer, complete with printer, modem and deeply discounted monthly Internet hook-up fees, for each of its 350,000 employees worldwide. In a National Public Radio interview, a company spokesperson said that potential advantages of this "fully wired workforce" included the fact that employees who left the workplace early to attend a child's ballet recital, for example, could catch up on missed work at home. Needless to say, our ears pricked up.

Any company that equips its employees with such 21st-century accouterments as PCs, cell phones, and various and sundry wireless devices — creating, as the buzzword goes, an eWorkforce — is poised to usher in a new work paradigm (whether they realize it or not). Once the means for flexibility are in place, can the ends be far behind?

Look for companies that have an overall philosophy of employee empowerment. Does the company you are considering have self-service (ESS) Intranet and/or HR call centers that help employees access critical human resources information (e.g. benefits, policies, vacation time accumulated)? Does it have a merit review process to which peers contribute? Does it offer incentive stock options and performance bonuses far down the hierarchy? In fact, has it jettisoned a steep hierarchy (a.k.a. a high-altitude adminisphere) for a flattened organization that rewards team effort? If the answer to at least some of these questions is yes, then this company is probably not averse to empowering employees in the area of flexibility, as well.

Search out companies that focus on employee retention. Some of these companies have human resources divisions specifically devoted to keeping valued employees content and, hence, loyal. As we already know, flexibility is one surefire way to achieve this.

Look for businesses that are truly customer-service oriented. In the long run, customers are more satisfied when an alert, on-the-ball workforce (a.k.a. one with many flexible positions) services them rather than a cadre of burnout candidates. Intelligent businesses understand this and will embrace flexibility in the name of enlightened self-interest. Besides, companies that really are customer-oriented will soon have to move toward 24/7 availability, if they haven't done so already. This in itself becomes a mandate for flexibility.

You may also want to think about companies with a global presence (the better to create a job share that functions across disparate time zones), but be sure to consider small start-ups, as well. Start-ups, which have no hard and fast rules that need to be bent and no adminisphere to scale, are often willing to accommodate flexibility in order to attract much-needed talent.

Is it truth or is it lip service?

When you are ready to go out on interviews, you will need to take a final savvy step toward getting what you want. You will need to ascertain if the flexible position for which you apply will actually be flexible once you get it. Unfortunately, we have heard more than a few horror stories about job candidates who landed a so-called "flexible" job one month and the next found themselves making frantic last-minute calls from the office trying to reschedule their child's birthday party because, they were told, they absolutely could not leave.

If you are not a careful listener, there is a possibility that you may accept a job only to find you did so with a completely different set of expectations for the job's parameters than your new employer. Over the next few weeks or months, a 24-hour permanent part-time position may, without your knowing quite how it happened, evolve into a 40-hour-a-week job, albeit with occasional early parole for good behavior on Friday afternoons.

So, <u>listen for qualifiers</u> when the flexible aspects of your job are discussed. If you are told that your proposed schedule will be fine "as long as you are available for extra time when we're busy," watch out. This is 21st-century America, and everyone is *always* busy.

<u>Get your agreed-upon hours in writing, with notations about specific exceptions</u>, e.g. "Will work 40 hours during the week of the such-and-such trade show" or "Will work full-time each March 15 — April 15 in preparation for tax filing."

Very importantly, <u>be sure to make your agreement with the hiring manager</u>. If you negotiate only with someone from human resources, you may find yourself tethered to a boss who doesn't buy into your plan at all.

Finally, <u>trust your instincts</u>. You have put a lot of time and effort toward getting the flexibility you need. If a first offer doesn't feel like it will work for you, try to hold out for one that will. In the meantime fine-tune your resume, hone your most marketable skills, keep your ears open and network like crazy. Before long, you will likely find what you're after.

Now for the next question: How will you make it work on a day-by-day basis? That's what the next chapter will address.

5

About Face: Making the Most of Less Face-Time

Once you have found a position that enables you to work flexibly, your life inside and outside of the office will improve immeasurably. Nevertheless, as with all change, a period of adjustment is to be expected.

You have now evolved from work "marathoner," plodding along mile after mile, to work "sprinter," exerting maximum compressed effort to meet your goals.

This chapter is meant to help you negotiate this evolution — during which you will truly come to understand the aphorism "work expands to fill the time allotted" — and help you fine-tune your arrangements so that both you and your employer will achieve maximum gains.

Halting erosion

In all of the issues we address in this chapter, you will note a common theme: Flexible employees must take proactive steps to ensure that the personal time for which they so carefully negotiated on paper is not eroded in practice. It's all well and good to make an agreement as to one's work arrangements. It's actually arranging those arrangements that can get tricky. Therefore, flexible employees must have the sanction of bosses, as well as the buy-in of subordinates and colleagues, regarding the details of any new partnership that has been forged with the company — for which, let us not forget, flexible employees have made substantial tradeoffs.

To start with, limits must be defined, set and enforced as to when flexible workers actually work. If employees have been contracted to walk out the door at 4 p.m., they must be prepared to do so — and their colleagues must be advised that this is the new norm. If a flexible employee's job description has been restructured, everyone who interacts with that employee should be aware of any amendments, so these can be honored. Moreover, if a job share has been created (as it should be in cases where a job truly demands full-time coverage), everyone affected needs to know which share partner is on call for what, and when.

We don't mean to suggest that malicious managers and crafty co-workers will deliberately set out to sabotage your flexible work arrangements unless things are spelled out. But one cannot underestimate the sheer force of habit. If the new ground rules aren't clear, people will likely default to old behavior simply because it is human nature to do so. Even the flexible employee may default, putting in extra hours and taking on more responsibilities than agreed to (and thus engaging in self-sabotage).

If the status quo remains unaltered, despite what may have been set down on paper, flexible employees might just walk out the door at the appointed stopping hour — and keep on walking. Sooner or later, resentment is bound to build to the point where it becomes intolerable. Then it's lose/lose, with employees abdicating what they worked so hard to achieve, and companies forfeiting the valued employees they tried so hard to retain. No one relishes such a scenario, and to avoid it we offer the following commonsense strategies.

Let's take a meeting — not

Regardless of the flexible option you have implemented, the most obvious and immediate change will be fewer hours per week spent interacting face to face with co-workers, subordinates and managers. When face-time diminishes, it stands to reason that other previously ingrained rites (some might say relics) of the typical day-to-day business agenda may go by the boards. First among these casualties is what we have come to think of as "the monster that ate the workday," a.k.a. the meeting.

When we asked job candidates what they considered to be the biggest hindrance to productivity in the traditional workday arrangement, the number one response was, not surprisingly, the dreaded meeting ritual. We use the word "ritual" because that's what most meetings are. They are little plays or pageants in which everyone seems to act out a specific role: the Curmudgeon, the Perennial Optimist, the Tsk-Tsking Number-Cruncher, the Suck-Up, the Cut-Up...well, you get the idea. Many, many times in the course of a week these ensemble productions unfold slowly and painfully, as the cast re-enacts scenarios in which they scold, question, second-guess, criticize, and (occasionally) even praise one another. During show time, important phone calls go unanswered, real work piles up, customers go ignored and zero value is added to the bottom line.

Moreover, there are preludes, postludes and intermissions attached to such events, during which everyone mills around and clusters into subgroups. Nearly as much time is given here to what was named by our candidates as the second biggest time-suck of the workday — namely, idle chitchat. Consequently, more work goes undone.

Ask employees and employers alike if most meetings are truly productive and they will likely reply with an eye-roll, a snort, or a similar expression roughly translating as, "Yeah, right." This sentiment is pretty much universal, yet one occasionally runs across an encouraging story, like the article in the *Wall Street Journal* about a large Wisconsin-based consumer goods company that mandated twice-a-month "Meeting-Free Fridays" for its 3,500 employees (with the darkened conference room sealed by the "No Meeting Day Police"). [1] Alas, most companies are not yet prepared to take the obvious step of curtailing the massive numbers of meetings that take place every day.

The flexible worker, however, must boldly lead the way, diplomatically declining to go where everyone else is going — i.e. to meetings, meetings and more meetings. Because, obviously enough, if one is in the office for a limited amount of time, it is all too easy for an even greater percentage of one's on-site time to be taken up with such fruitless endeavors than when one is traditionally scheduled. As a flexibly scheduled employee who needs to extract maximum effectiveness from each hour on the job, you will have to determine which meetings are critical for you to attend and which are not. Then you will need to convince your boss of the wisdom of your choices.

As a rule of thumb, we believe that <u>no one should attend a meeting unless they have something of value to contribute or learn that could not otherwise be contributed or learned in a more efficient manner.</u>

At first thought you might imagine this rules out your attendance at all meetings for all time, but that's not necessarily the case. There are some processes that actually benefit from meeting time. One productive type of meeting is the ad hoc brainstorming session at which attendees focus on an immediate concern and emerge with a consensus and an action plan. Another is the informational/bonding meeting of the sort that occurs when a company's sales reps from around the country visit headquarters or some off-site locale for an annual or semi-annual conference. These gatherings are important less for their ability to disseminate, say, new product information (which, after all, could be done via corporate Intranet or teleconferencing) than for their ability to reinforce *esprit de corps* among far-flung employees. In this case, the idle chitchat that takes place can actually be beneficial.

You'll also want to attend any meeting where a personal pitch on your part — and nothing short of it — will result in achieving a desired objective, e.g. a 25 percent budget increase for your department's R&D next year. In addition, long-term planning and strategy sessions can be useful if they don't routinely deteriorate into grandstanding displays by a few "cast members." But beware if these meetings tend to pop up on your agenda more than once or twice a year. We know all too many organizations where mid-to-top-level executives spend nearly all their time either traveling to and from, attending, or preparing to present at such convocations.

Above all, do everything you can to extricate yourself from the true kiss-of-death gatherings — those week-in, week-out staples (be they staff meetings, marketing meetings or get-togethers with other seemingly innocuous names) that take place whether or not there is anything new or even remotely relevant to discuss. These are the black holes of meetings, into which one may disappear indefinitely, perhaps entering another dimension altogether.

As for lunch meetings with clients, important contacts, and so on, we admit that breaking bread can help build and strengthen relationships. Eating, for most of us, is associated with positive feelings of trust and security. The problem with these, however, is that while you consume two or three courses — leaving shoptalk for coffee time, as is considered polite — most of your day is consumed, as well. While we believe there are occasions that warrant lunch meetings, we suggest you book such events sparingly. Dining meetings are useful for mending fences if there is a particular problem or misunderstanding. They can also prove worthwhile in the long run if the time is consciously devoted to learning more about, for instance, a prospective new hire than a mere resume can convey. In these situations, it may be hard to measure the bottom-line value in terms of a day's productivity; nevertheless, the long-term payoff will eventually be evident.

As a flexible employee, you must judiciously decide which meetings are worth your time. Then you need to decide how you will catch up on any relevant developments that were presented in meetings you did not attend, whether by reading a recap memo or debriefing a colleague who was there (preferably one who remained awake). You should also have someone in your department who can represent and speak for you at certain meetings. Once you figure this out, present a brief but comprehensive plan to your direct report manager. Focusing on productivity as your goal, explain why you don't think it's wise for you to warm one of those conference table seats more than absolutely necessary.

Leftovers

When you have reduced your meeting time, you are free to maximize the hours you spend working. Whether the bulk of your work is done on site or out of the office, freedom from meetings gives you power to accomplish more in less time. As a result, even though you are showing less face, your increased productivity should actually lighten the load of your co-workers. Nevertheless, it's naïve to assume that the universe will arrange itself so that issues regarding your various projects, clients, and so on, will arise only when you are around. The flexible worker must always have a Plan B (and C and D) so "leftovers" may be dealt with in an efficient manner. (By the way, traditionally scheduled employees also have issues that arise when they are not around — often when they are stuck in or on their way to a meeting. But no one is going to question the validity of the 40-hour week because of it. Flexible employees, on the other hand, are held to a higher degree of accountability.)

Our first suggestion is that from the start you schedule your days in the office to coincide with the times known to be the busiest and most demanding of your input. This, of course, varies from industry to industry, company to company, and department to department. But if, say, you work for a publication that is put to bed on Wednesdays, you obviously want to be around on Wednesdays. If you head a customer-service call center where phones ring off the hook on Monday mornings, you will certainly need to have a ringside seat for the mayhem. If it's unclear exactly when your department's busiest times are, it might be worthwhile to put some effort into tracking things like the number of incoming phone calls before deciding which days your presence is most required and when you can be most easily spared.

Your colleagues will appreciate any effort you make to be nearby when things are at their most hectic. But that alone won't keep the occasional crunch or crisis from taking place in your absence. Therefore, we also offer the following suggestions.

- Keep your files — both computer files and paper ones — well organized and well labeled. Be sure everything has a name, a date, and an indication as to whether it is complete or "in the works." Purge the files periodically so they do not become cluttered.

- Once you have done the above, walk several of your co-workers (including, of course, your job-share partner if you have one) through your system, making sure they can locate key files and documents easily.

- Make sure several people are aware of your computer screen name and passwords, so they are not thwarted when they need to retrieve vital information. (Obviously, if you have sensitive or confidential information, put appropriate safeguards in place.)

- Advise your clients and contacts who else in your office is capable of answering questions and/or making decisions if you are not there. Be certain to reassure them that, as brilliant as you are, you are surrounded by very capable colleagues.

The preceding steps will not only help your co-workers and assuage your clients, but will also prevent you from receiving a plethora of "where the heck is such-and-such?" phone calls. Of course, you know what they say about the best-laid plans. Even the most obsessed organizer is bound to discover it's impossible to think of everything ahead of time. Stuff happens, after all, because that's the nature of life. Hence some urgent calls are bound to come your way.

Which leads us to our next topic. We have already pointed out that the flexible worker must plan to be available when he or she is off site. But here's the million-dollar question: Just how much availability is reasonable — and when does an always-available attitude start to border on self-abuse?

I told you not to call me here

Hail, technology! It has enabled the wonderful phenomenon of flexibility. Cell phones and pagers and, increasingly, wireless devices and company Intranet portals, have freed us from the shackles of an all face, all the time workplace. We like and appreciate communication technology, for it is good. Having said that, we can appreciate the downside of being contactable on a 24/7 basis. Flexible employees, and indeed all employees and employers, must understand that at some point, for any given individual, the workday must conclude.

But just when should that be? Having access to a flexible employee during the course of a company's customary business hours may seem entirely reasonable. But to make life easier, both for these employees and those who need to reach them, we suggest implementing a two-tiered procedure.

First, for routine communications, special check-in times should be established. If your department members know you will be checking your e-mail and voicemail at 11 a.m. and 3 p.m. each day, they will quickly develop the habit of structuring their communications to you accordingly. For urgent situations in which your immediate input is needed, be sure that a select few of your colleagues have a means of reaching you at times other than your regular check-ins, until the usual close of business.

This still leaves the question of after-hours emergencies. For these, each of you in your various professions must come to an agreement with your co-workers and your manager as to <u>what constitutes a genuine emergency</u>. If you are a cardiac surgeon this is likely a pretty easy question to answer, since your emergencies are literally life-and-death situations. But what if you are a computer programmer? Is it an emergency when an entire system goes down and only you have the codes to reboot? (In which case, we might ask, why doesn't anyone else have the codes?) What if you are a sales rep, a publicist, a graphic designer, an accountant or a benefits administrator? Is there really all that much that can't wait until morning? You will need to reach a consensus on this and set boundaries accordingly, perhaps with a paging system that ranks emergencies as a "1" ("the future of the company hangs in the balance"), a "2" ("we could really, really use some help here"), or a "3" ("please give us a shout if you're not tied up").

As of this writing, at least 41 percent of employers outfit some of their workers with cell phones or pagers, and this number will surely grow rapidly. [2] Without appropriate limits, however, communications abuse will be rampant. In fact, some companies have already recognized the danger. (Intel has gone so far as to offer workshops that encourage employees to tell supervisors to stop calling them at home at night. [3]) Clearly, availability is one of those issues where the flexible workforce can lead the way to saner, more humane working conditions for all.

Workplace etiquette

Now we come to something a bit "softer" but of equal importance. On the surface, the topic is workplace etiquette. But it's really about emotional intelligence on the job — and why we believe flexible employees must embody the essence of workplace "EQ."

It has always been a good idea to be civil — indeed, to be kind — to one's fellow employees. Why would we want to alienate anyone upon whom we depend so greatly and with whom we interact so frequently? But in today's competitive, stressful business environment — and in office spaces that are increasingly open and non-private — common courtesies are, more than ever, a saving grace. They go a long way toward building team spirit and easing tensions.

Obviously, everyone should observe workplace niceties. Career counselors strongly suggest, for example, avoiding office faux pas such as eavesdropping, making unnecessary noise, acting secretive, being overly intrusive, and even wearing perfumes or after-shaves that are too strong. [4] These are offenses to which no one ought to plead guilty, regardless of how many hours they work. There are, however, a few additional suggestions we feel are particularly applicable to flexible employees.

My desk is your desk

The first has to do with shared workstations. Shared workstations are, in general, becoming a more common phenomenon. AT&T, for example, determined that — for certain groups of employees — up to a half-dozen people could share the same desk and equipment formerly assigned to one person. As of this writing, they had approximately 14,000 employees in shared workstation arrangements. [5]

Shared workstations are not only for flexibly scheduled employees. Sometimes they accommodate others, such as employees who travel frequently. But as a flexible employee, chances are good you may be one of the many who will hang your hat on, say, Tuesdays and Thursdays where someone else hangs his on Mondays, Wednesdays and Fridays.

Not surprisingly, career-counselor advice with regard to this sounds very much like the advice we all got from our mothers: Don't make a mess and always pick up after yourself. Your desk partner, whether he or she is your job-share partner or a regular colleague, needs to access essential tools and information without having to rummage through mounds of clutter. In our own random survey of office desk drawers we unearthed such items as breath mints, lip balms, contact lens solutions, CDs, family photos, ancient to-do lists, Gordian knots of rubber bands and paper clips, chopsticks, drinking straws, packs of gum, expired library cards, and broken reading glasses. If this sounds familiar, a rigorous purging is in order.

Certainly, individuals who share desks may devise their own rules for peaceful coexistence, agreeing perhaps that the lower left-hand drawer is mine and the lower right-hand drawer is exclusively yours. If so, such agreements should be consistently honored, with sundry knickknacks stored accordingly and a "no peeking" policy firmly adhered to. At the end of one's on-site time, desks should be cleared of non-work-related materials as well as any work-related materials not specifically being left for a desk partner's attention.

As for computers, your workstation partners won't appreciate clutter on the screen desktop any more than they do on the actual desktop. Keep your computer files segregated into personalized folders. Always give your partners fair warning and obtain their buy-in if you are going to install software upgrades or otherwise tamper with applications. And if you've installed an amusing new screen saver, remember that one person's amusement may be another's annoyance. Finally, at the end of your day be sure the PC is properly shut down.

Minimize the personal

Career counselors point out that it's impolite to expose colleagues to the intimate details of one's personal life. This can prove difficult when you spend a five-day, 40-hour week in an office, since many personal matters don't neatly segment themselves to fall outside of the 9-to-5 schedule. (Try, for instance, reaching your dentist or your child's school principal after 6 p.m.)

Emergencies aside, flexible workers must adhere to a stricter rule of thumb. Having made the effort to alter his or her work-life balance, a flexibly scheduled employee should also make every effort to shield work hours from family dramas and other personal affairs. Realistically, this may not always be possible, but it is certainly less <u>im</u>possible than for someone on a traditional schedule.

Besides, as we've already pointed out, flexible employees are, at least at this point in time, held to a higher standard. If flexible workers give their bosses or colleagues reason to complain, it's all too easy for people to say, "Aha! This flexibility thing doesn't seem to be working out."

Face it

Clearly there are advantages to showing less face around the office. We have detailed ways to ease the transition to less face-time for those not used to such a phenomenon, so that the advantages ultimately outweigh any disadvantages. Having said that, just because all face, all the time is unproductive, let's not rule out some face-time as necessary.

Flexible workers need, now and again, to show up, make eye contact, shake some hands, share some laughs, commiserate and *kibbitz* with colleagues. On the most fundamental level, humans will always crave contact with one another. No technology can obliterate this need, and for that we should be grateful.

People are important. In fact, they are the most important resource of any business. It will be to the benefit of all if even the speediest "sprinter" stops for breath long enough to respectfully hear out a colleague with a question, a customer with a gripe, or a subordinate with a good idea. Employees should never be so literal about the meaning of productivity that they rush imprudently or lose patience when such a virtue is most required.

As for flexibility, we trust it will enable more and more employees to not only make the most of their face-time, but to present their colleagues with a face that has a heartfelt smile on it.

6

The Home Front Challenge: The Ins and Outs of Working at Home

"Knock, knock."
"Who's there?"
"OSHA."
"OSHA who?"
"Oh, sure, ya like working at home. But can we come in and have a look around?"

❖   ❖   ❖   ❖   ❖

All right, go ahead and groan. But for a while there the prospect of OSHA (the Occupational Safety and Health Administration of the U.S. government's Labor Department) entering the home-based offices of telecommuters and other workers, in search of potentially hazardous conditions, was no joke.

In the first week of January 2000, just as we were breathing a sigh of relief that Y2K had passed without incident, OSHA rocked the world of telecommuters and the companies that employ them when one of its advisories came to public attention. The advisory indicated that companies allowing employees to work at home are responsible for safety violations that occur at the home work-site.[1] Although the advisory (actually a letter of guidance to one particular employer, Texas-based CSC Credit) did not offer specifics, it seemed to imply that employers would be responsible for making sure off-site employees had ergonomically correct furniture, proper lighting, heating, and ventilation systems. Further, interpreters inferred that employers would need to train these employees to comply with the full range of OSHA standards.

Uproar ensued, and speculation ran rampant as to OSHA's true intent. America's 19.6 million telecommuters, not to mention millions of other employees who occasionally worked from home, wondered whether federal inspectors would come a-knocking, asking to see if their desk chairs had lumbar support or if their electrical outlets were overloaded. Would employers now have free rein to come snooping around their houses under the pretense of preventing carpal tunnel syndrome?

Employers, for their part, worried about liability issues. They envisioned being sued if their telecommuting employees had so much as a run-in with a doorjamb on their way to answering a ringing telephone.

Across the land, irate working folk and befuddled business owners alike flooded radio talk show lines and penned furious letters to their local newspapers and congressional representatives. As one telecommuter we had recently placed in what she said was her dream job put it: "My dream is turning into a nightmare. This sounds like Brave New World and Kakfa all rolled into one."

In light of similar sentiments, OSHA backpedaled.

A few days after the organization's dictum began drawing widespread scrutiny, then Labor Secretary Alexis Herman announced she was withdrawing the federal interpretation letter. Citing "widespread confusion and unintended consequences," she insisted the advisory was informal and not intended to be taken as a policy statement for the entire business community. [2] Further, she offered assurances that there were, as of that moment in time, "no rules, no liability" regarding home offices, and that "the federal government has neither the desire nor the resources to investigate private homes." [3] Herman did add, however, that important questions had been raised, and that an inter-agency task force would be convened to conduct a long-term study of the issues involved.

Even after the retraction, the phones at Flexible Resources, which had been ringing with media queries since the moment the story hit the airwaves, refused to be silent. Without meaning to (obviously!) OSHA had pushed a hot button at the heart of the zeitgeist. Clearly, more and more companies and employees were moving in the direction of telecommuting, and now everyone wanted to debate what the rules of the game might ultimately become.

For our part, we were glad to see that the government recognizes telecommuting as a viable work option. And, of course, we were only too happy to contribute to the public discourse.

Let common sense prevail

First of all, we want to reiterate that we are wholly in favor of telecommuting. Its numerous advantages for employees include stress reduction, commuter cost-savings, and increased opportunities to spend time no longer wasted travelling to and from work on other endeavors (such as family togetherness, community service, and the pursuit of individual avocations). Its advantages for employers include a happier and more loyal workforce, a significant recruiting advantage, an opportunity to increase productivity by reducing sick days and tardiness, an opportunity to increase efficiency by spreading a workforce across time zones, and a reduced reliance on expensive office space.

Secondly, we want to point out that telecommuting is becoming increasingly popular. Of the 2,700 Sun Microsystems employees who responded to a survey in the autumn of 2000, nearly 80 percent said they worked from home part of the time. And half of all Cisco Systems employees work at home at least one day a week. [4]

But can working from home be dangerous? Sure, if certain common-sense practices are overlooked. Nevertheless, we know one thing for certain: Even if telecommuters worked in backyard tree houses during thunderstorms, they still wouldn't face the same statistical perils they do each time they get behind the wheel of their cars for the long drive to the office.

Okay, okay, we don't really endorse working in a backyard tree house. Or in a basement beneath a leaky pipe. Or in an unventilated closet. What we do endorse is employer-employee cooperation and the application of commonsense procedures to telecommuting-related issues. Specifically:

- Management should insist that the home office is indeed a proper office — with a door that closes. Forget the dining-room table. The telecommuter needs a clean, quiet, uncluttered space in order to be productive.

- The company should ensure that the home office is equipped with the same type of technology the employee would have in the office, including a computer with modem, voicemail, fax, etc.

- The home office should have a separate phone line that family members do not use.

- It should be spelled out in advance specifically what the company will purchase in terms of equipment and supplies. (Consultants usually buy their own equipment and supplies and consider it a cost of doing business; staffers may well prefer other arrangements.)

- The company and the telecommuter should establish ground rules for when, how and how often both sides will communicate. They should also agree as to when, if at all, the employee is required to report to the office.

- Management should also lay down rules about childcare. We advise all candidates who are telecommuting for the first time that this arrangement is not a way to save on babysitting costs.

Who's that knocking at my door?

How will all this be implemented and enforced? Certain firms with large and established telecommuting workforces actually have consultants on staff to assist off-site employees in setting up home offices according to company specifications. But many companies only offer guidelines, and then trust employees to use their heads.

It's not that the latter sort of companies care any less about the well-being of telecommuters. Their lack of hands-on assistance can actually be chalked up to a number of factors. The first of these is logistics. Arranging for furnishings to be moved into an employee's home is challenging enough — not to mention the extra challenge of moving it back out should that employee resign or be terminated. Another roadblock is expense. The combined cost of a work surface, storage cabinet and chair can easily run anywhere from one to two thousand dollars. Many companies feel that supplying a computer and other work-related tools is essential (a 1991 American Management Association survey of nearly 1,300 respondents revealed that 51 percent of telecommuters had employers that loaned or purchased such equipment on their behalf). [5] But some of these companies also feel their employees can make do without an influx of new home furnishings.

Yet another stumbling block is employee resistance. Let's face it: Not everyone relishes the idea of company consultants mucking about in their home — and imposing a potentially incompatible interior-design scheme — any more than they relish the notion of the Feds barging in for a surprise OSHA inspection. (By the way, we believe the Labor Department when they insist they have no plans for becoming Telecommuting Police. They don't have the wherewithal to pull it off, and — as we've already witnessed — the public relations problem would be immense.)

If both employer and employee have enough mutual trust to arrange a home workspace under the auspices of general guidelines, so be it. To quote a colleague of ours who recently set up his own home office: "There was no rocket science needed to figure out that investing in a sturdy, adjustable chair — as opposed to unearthing a collapsible beach slingback from my basement — was a good prescription for avoiding back pain." Likewise, MENSA membership is not required to determine that if the lights dim every time a piece of equipment is turned on, then the electrical wiring needs to be rethought. As with all work-related matters, we believe that if everyone simply behaves responsibly, things will work out even better than anticipated.

Spotting televacationers

Before we leave the notion of Telecommuting Police entirely, there's another issue we want to address, and that's the issue of home workers' privacy with regard to their employers.

In general, when employees accept a job they give up certain rights to privacy while on that job. This doesn't mean employers can put videocams in the rest rooms or monitor the fat content of one's lunch; it does mean they may adopt e-mail and telephone policies which preclude the use of electronic mail and phone lines for non-business-related purposes.

As with all things, common sense and common courtesy should underlie the enforcement of such policies. Employers generally don't mind if employees make a few calls home during the course of a day, or take a minute to check out an online weather report. (At any rate, spending a great deal of time hunting down such minor diversions is a spectacular waste of resources.) But employees who spend the bulk of their on-the-job hours Net-surfing, circulating e-mail jokes or chatting with distant friends and relations are, obviously, abusing their privileges. They will not be able to pull it off for too long, of course, because the bottom line is that precious little work will be accomplished.

The same principles ought to apply at home. Telecommuters should be just as aware — and respectful — of telephone and e-mail policies as are in-house workers, and equally careful about how much time they spend browsing non-job-related Web sites. Once again, some latitude is reasonable. But all in all, the employer's expectation should be that work time will be spent working and that job-related equipment will be used for job-related purposes.

Many employees bristle at the prospect of an employer's use of certain types of electronic surveillance — including e-mail filters that monitor particular keywords — which are becoming increasingly available. At the same time, many of our candidates who wish to telecommute have asked us how their bosses will know they're actually working "when they can't see me or drop by my office?" Indeed, many managers have asked us the same question.

We understand that there are people unable to shake the image of someone allegedly working at home who's secretly blending up an International Coffee mix and kicking back with *Days of Our Lives*. But we can tell you what will prevent such transgressions: It's not the honor system, it's not expensive electronic peeping, and it's not military — style surprise inspections. Once again, it's plain old common sense.

What's the real test of whether or not someone is working at home? It's the same as in the office, of course. The proof is in the pudding. Is the work getting done, or not?

Sure, there is a chance that a telecommuter will slack off, take advantage and devolve into a televacationer. It's about the same chance that someone in an office will while away their days behind a desk by balancing their checkbook, forwarding joke e-mails, or visiting Internet chat rooms to discuss extraterrestrial abductions. Such employees, alas, are not as anomalous as we would like to think, but we all know they do not last long. Neither does (or should) an indolent home-based worker.

Once again we should point out that, fairly or not, a flexible employee who telecommutes will most likely be held to a higher standard than an on-site worker when it comes to meeting deadlines, making quotas, and exhibiting other measures of productivity. A public relations account manager who telecommutes two days a week and works on site another two days explained it this way. "On the days when I am in the office, I sometimes lose valuable hours to redundant meetings, co-workers' chitchat and other miscellaneous interruptions — from dealing with the Xerox repairman to sorting out lunch orders. If not much actual work is accomplished by close of business, though, everyone seems to accept it was 'just one of those days.' But when I come in from a day at home, I'm expected to produce the press releases I wrote, the lists of editors I pitched over the phone, and so on. And if I said it was 'just one of those days,' I suspect my telecommuting career would be short-lived."

She's right, of course. No one ever said life was fair.

Family ties

Trust is a key element in any employer-employee relationship, and especially so when something new and untried is being implemented. We have implicit faith that the American workforce is truly coming of age, and that employers will treat their employees like the grownups they are and give them the degree of autonomy they require.

But will everyone else be so understanding?

Sometimes workers who attempt to do all or part of their work at home find that their biggest challenge is getting those on the home front to truly understand the concept. While employers with telecommuting employees emphatically — and rightfully — state that such arrangements are not a substitute for childcare, one's children may initially disagree. There may also be an issue with one's spouse, often so enthused to have their partner home at lunchtime that they thoughtfully prepare a three-course meal or (perhaps less thoughtfully) suggest Monday morning might be a good time to plant the begonias or re-shingle the roof.

The pull of family ties can be strong; of this there is no doubt. Nevertheless, telecommuters must be able to set firm boundaries between home office and home life.

Having a door that shuts is one thing. But can a work-at-home parent keep the kids from knocking on it? Undoubtedly they'll want to pay Mom or Dad a visit or two. Perhaps they'll ask to swivel around on a desk chair, or request the use of the computer to visit cartoonnetwork.com. Sometimes they'll just want to show off a drawing they made. Sometimes they'll feel compelled to tattle on a sibling they believe should be shipped off to reform school.

Realistically, interruptions are a fact of life. But it is imperative to set ground rules and then to allow for exceptions and extenuating circumstances as needed.

School-age children often long to see a parent when they return home, even if it's just for a few minutes before they set off to play or tackle their homework. A little break set aside at this time of day will go a long way toward satiating their parent-cravings (and your kid-cravings) until work is done. "Let's face it," said a telecommuting mom we know. "If I were at the office, there would be at least 15 or 20 minutes in the course of the afternoon that would be devoted to refueling in an informal coffee klatch. At home, I set that time aside for a milk-and-cookies break with my seven-year-old and nine-year-old. Sure, there are times when I have to work through that period of the day, but I try to schedule carefully so I can catch up with the kids at some point. If I do, they are happy to go play or start homework until my quitting time. In the long run it's emotionally good for all of us, and good for getting in my final hour or two of work uninterrupted."

For younger children, it's imperative to have a sitter at home with whom they are comfortable. It's definitely not a good idea to hire a sitter who starts the same day that one's telecommuting job begins. Give everyone time to get used to one another beforehand, and try to schedule things so there is always an overlap between parent and caregiver at the start of each day.

As for selecting caregivers, choose wisely. They need to be skilled at keeping little ones who are prone to wandering down the hall toward the home office otherwise occupied. The sitter should be independent-minded, as opposed to someone always prompting the tykes to "Go ask Mommy or Dad."

But let's face it. Even Mary Poppins might not be able to distract your children completely when you are in proximity. There will be times when you simply have to be firm. Explain — as best you can, and in an age-appropriate way — just what it is you are doing in that mysterious room down the hall or up the stairs. And let them know why what you do is important. Try not to scare them ("My boss will kill me if I don't get this done!") or threaten them with poverty ("If I don't work there won't be any money for toys, ever!"). But do explain that your work is satisfying and interesting — and that people are counting on you to do your share. It wouldn't hurt, either, to remind the kids that working at home actually does mean you get to spend more time with them, and less time on the highway.

Kids, of course, aren't the only potential flies in a telecommuter's ointment. Sometimes grownups, too, need reality checks. Friendly (perhaps a tad too friendly) neighbors need to be discouraged from dropping by for morning coffee or a late-afternoon sociable, if such visits fall within one's scheduled work hours. PTA zealots must be informed in no uncertain terms that your telecommuting obligations do not allow for bake sale duty or field trip chaperoning. And, as we can personally attest, everyone within range must be trained not to do you any favors by bringing in FedEx packages left on the front porch. Why? Because these are invariably your outgoing packages and such well-meant "assistance" will have you chasing the FedEx truck down the street, screaming like a banshee.

As for spouses, we're sorry to say they often need a little nudge in the right direction (that direction being <u>out</u> of your office). In theory, one's husband or wife — especially if he or she also works — should be better equipped than young children to comprehend a telecommuter's exceedingly limited availability during work hours. But sometimes they have to be ever so gently reminded that, no, this would not be a good time to apply for a home equity loan, plan next summer's vacation, or upload digital pictures of the kids onto the hard drive.

Likewise, spouses who work outside the home often need de-programming when it comes to their belief that family members who telecommute should undertake a large portion of the household chores because they are, after all, "home all day." An anecdote relayed to us by a marketing executive who segued from working at her office five days a week to telecommuting for three of those five days — but still working full-time — typifies the misunderstandings that can occur.

"My husband had what I call the 'Dry Cleaning Fantasy.' He didn't share this with me when my new work arrangement began, but apparently he assumed that since I was 'around the house' Wednesday through Friday, I would pick up the dry cleaning more frequently and do lots of other errands that we previously had saved up for Saturday marathons. One Thursday night he frowned and asked me where his shirts were. I could not imagine what he meant, until he explained his bit of wishful thinking. Needless to say, we had to have a little chat."

The best time to address such issues with children, friends and spouses is not during work hours, when one's time — and temper — can be short. It is, in fact, during downtime when touchy matters can be examined at greater length. But here's the rub: That, of course, presumes one even allows for downtime.

This brings us to the most important boundary-setting issue of all — the boundary telecommuters must set for themselves. Sometimes when one works at home it is all too easy to forget that one also lives there. The door to the office shuts both ways. You can close it behind you when you go in, to keep interruptions at bay. But you must also close it behind you when you leave, as a reminder that the day's work is done.

The telecommuting personality

In an earlier chapter we discussed some of the ideal personality characteristics of the flexible employee. Now let's look at the characteristics which, very specifically, apply to people who can work contentedly and productively as telecommuters.

Chief among these is the ability to decompress from the workday relatively quickly, reentering the world of home and family without carrying in all of work's baggage.

Stress is contagious, as most of us know, and work-related stress not left on the job can severely impact one's spouse and children. A recent study of more than a thousand children of working parents found that about a third actively expressed the wish that their parents would be less stressed from work. 6 Many of them said they looked for "mood clues" when their moms and dads walked in the door, to see if it was safe to approach without getting their heads bitten off. To avoid the head-biting scenario, some people use drive time — figuratively as well as literally — to shift gears and refocus from a corporate to a domestic agenda. By the time they enter their house they are anxious for a recap of their loved ones' day, a hug from the kids and an enthusiastic slurp from the dog. Telecommuters do not have this built-in segue, and while the upside is significant (no traffic to battle, less gas to guzzle), there is also a bit of a mixed blessing to factor in.

If you are not able to switch from employee hat to parent hat in a millisecond, don't assume you can't pull off telecommuting. Instead, make an effort to methodically factor in a few minutes for the decompression ritual of your choice before morphing into your other key role. Consider turning off the computer and the phone, dimming the lights (perhaps even lighting a candle) and engaging in some stretching and/or meditation exercises before you emerge from the home office at the workday's conclusion. If this sounds too mellow, try popping a CD into your PC and letting your favorite music serve as a mood-altering device.

Another personality characteristic especially useful for telecommuters is what psychologists term "freedom from distractibility." This is just what it sounds like — a knack for concentrating pretty much exclusively on the task at hand. No matter how physically close they may be to the fireside fray of home, telecommuters must manifest the equivalent of aural and emotional blinders while on the job. They must resist the temptation to investigate every laugh, shout, bark, thud or other bit of onomatopoeia emanating from the family room, and repress those urges to "just pop out and see what the gang is up to." Except for scheduled breaks and genuine emergencies, the successful telecommuter must enter "the zone" while in the home office, bringing all energies to bear on servicing the client on the phone and perfecting that memo on the screen.

If you are a natural when it comes to freedom from distractibility, chances are you know it. You were the kind of college student who could complete a term paper while your roommate blasted heavy metal and/or conducted a tempestuous love affair on the other bed. You can read a novel at the beach while your children are burying you in sand. And you can probably remember dozens of important telephone numbers (even backward, if you tried) without consulting your Rolodex. If such feats aren't your strong suit, there are certain tricks that can help "up" your non-distractibility index, like wearing earplugs that drown out the joyful noise of family, or posting a sign on the inside of your door that asks, "Shouldn't I really be working?"

Finally, we highly recommend that telecommuters exhibit a lack of defensiveness about their work arrangements. Some people are so paranoid that bosses or co-workers will question their level of contribution that they overcompensate by checking e-mail every two minutes or sending cyber-messages in the wee hours of the morning, just to prove they are "on the job." This sort of behavior creates unnecessary stress and sets dangerous precedents by raising the bar too high. What seems like extra effort on the home-based worker's part will soon become routine to those on the receiving end of these fevered messages. Co-workers and managers may actually come to expect every-two-minute communication, and woe is the telecommuter on the day this fails to occur. Our advice: chill. Remember, televacationers will be found out; workers who are truly on the job need only live up to reasonable expectations — not superhuman ones.

Telework centers

Perhaps this chapter has awakened you to the possibility that working at home might be an ideal circumstance for you. But perhaps it has alerted you to the fact that it may not be your cup of tea. If the latter is true, there's no reason to hang your head in shame. Nor is there any reason to assume you'll be forced to spend the rest of your days enduring long rush-hour commutes. There is, in fact, another option, one that combines what some consider the best of both worlds: the telework center.

Telework centers are office hubs — complete with all necessary equipment, furnishings and technology — flung far afield from the home office, usually in or near populous suburbs that are home to numerous employees of a given company. Such centers, which have been utilized for a number of years by federal employees, are catching on in the private sector with companies such as Lockheed Martin, Charles Schwab and Sun Microsystems. Sometimes called drop-in centers, they are well-suited for employees that wish to avoid long commutes all or part of the time but still desire or require a group environment in which to do their jobs. In many cases, employees work out of these facilities a few days a week, going into the main office on the remaining days. In some cases, however, employees work only part of the day in a telework center — waiting, for example, for traffic to thin before completing their commute.

Telework centers offer obvious advantages for road-weary, time-deprived employees, and they may be the ideal solution for people who — for any combination of personal and/or practical reasons — like the idea of working close to home better than the thought of actually working at home. Employers, too, can reap rewards by creating this type of workspace. Ann

Bamesberger, Sun Microsystem's director of workplace effectiveness, sums these up nicely when she explains: "Instead of chasing space, we're chasing people. Instead of thinking, 'Where can we get a big chunk of land?' we're thinking, 'Where do people want to work?'"

Not everyone who works in a telework center is a flexibly scheduled employee, but clearly such facilities will continue to empower flexible options as they become more and more widespread. We believe we are seeing the beginning of a significant trend in this regard, and for this we are thankful. The workplace must be reinvented, and any innovation along these lines is reason for optimism.

❖ ❖ ❖ ❖ ❖

In this chapter we have examined the advantages and challenges of working at (or near) home. In this entire section of the book, we have examined — from the employee's point of view — strategies and guidelines for obtaining, fine-tuning and making the most of flexible employment opportunities.

In the following section, we will switch our perspective and focus on the challenges and rewards of flexibility from the managerial point of view. We hope those of you who have been intrigued by *The End Of Work As We Know It* thus far will keep on reading. Surely everyone in the workplace can benefit from multiple perspectives. And besides, as time goes on we fully expect more flexible workers will be hired for and promoted into managerial positions. There is no time like the present to prepare.

PART III

The Flexibility Formula — A Guide for Managers

"Sane scheduling, sane supervision and continual communication."

—Nadine Mockler and Laurie Young,
The End of Work As We Know It

7

Why is this Manager Smiling? Managing the Flexible Workplace

Remember the Rip Van Worker hypothesis with which we began this book? In it, an employee who'd slumbered for five years awoke to find the workplace transformed. As a result of his company's embrace of flexible employment options, virtually every aspect of this worker's day was less stressful — from his accelerated commute to the lack of pointless meetings. Even better, his company's stock was up, its competitive edge was strong, and his fellow employees were productive and content. But let's not forget one of Rip Van Worker's most striking observations: His department manager, Bob, had been transformed, as well. No longer a high-strung, overtired grump, he had been reborn as an upbeat, chipper and uncharacteristically calm fellow.

Why was Manager Bob smiling? You would be smiling, too, if your numbers were up, your customers were more satisfied, your employee attrition was down, and you were attracting top new talent to your organization. And, in fact, you will be smiling when the inevitable future unfolds and many of the people you manage are empowered to perform their jobs under saner, more sensible conditions.

Feeling skeptical? We don't blame you. But in the 13 years we've been contributing to the evolution of a flexible workplace, we have witnessed the conversion of hundreds of formerly skeptical managers. These same managers now appreciate the remarkable value that flexibility adds to their departments and divisions, not to mention the day-to-day ease added to their lives as the morale and output of those that they manage skyrockets.

We know there's a part of you that wants to believe us (or you wouldn't be reading this), but we also understand that any major change in the status quo is frightening. After all, the universality of flexible options does in fact constitute the end of work as we know it. Skepticism and a certain degree of dread are only natural in the face of revolutionary change, regardless of its potential or its promise.

This chapter is meant to assuage your fears by examining the benefits and challenges of flexibility from a practical perspective. We want to assure you that the advent of flexibility is not just another managerial burden for you to bear. Nor is the flexible workplace one more flavor-of-the-month corporate trend. In fact, as you will see, transitioning to a flexible workplace can be virtually seamless, because the guiding philosophy behind it is common sense.

Flexibility truly represents unparalleled opportunity. What's more, it is here to stay, because it is evolving organically out of demographic, technological and sociological changes that are, quite simply, irreversible.

You may work for, or ultimately join, a company that already embraces flexibility to some degree; or you may be part of an organization that has some catching up to do. Either way, your job will go infinitely more smoothly if you understand what flexible employees can do for you and what you as a manager can do for them.

Daily blessings

Let's get back to Smiling Bob for a bit, and look at how his day-to-day life at the office was altered in our hypothetical example. As wonderful as flexibility proved for his company overall, Bob's personality metamorphosis from a jittery Type A to a mellow Type B didn't happen solely because of the big picture and the bottom line. It occurred because of a combination of factors that made his daily responsibilities easier to perform while altering the ambience of the environment in which he performed them.

Let's face it. Managing a bunch of people, each with his or her disparate needs, concerns and temperaments, is just plain hard. Empowering those people to meet many of their own needs via flexible scheduling removes much of the angst from the equation.

Before Manager Bob's company embraced flexibility, he had a serious problem with department members who were obviously over-fatigued — and whose job performances suffered as a result. Bob was sympathetic. He knew that long commutes at peak travel times, combined with rigidly scheduled work hours and an abundance of family and community commitments, caused many of the people he worked with to log far fewer than the recommended eight hours of sleep per night. (Statistically, he'd read, about a third of them were logging less than six and a half hours. [1])

But, as said, job performance was obviously suffering, and Bob was in a bind. Countless lapses in memory and seemingly careless errors among people who were normally sharp as tacks when <u>not</u> sleep-deprived were taking their toll. Bob knew that some companies had gone as far as creating on-site nap rooms to cope with similar dilemmas, and he wondered if that might be the solution. Once flexibility came along, however, the sleep-deprivation problem all but vanished. Bob's department was literally humming with energy. Mistakes declined as output surged. Moods improved and tempers flared less often.

Another of Bob's dilemmas before the advent of flexibility was figuring out how to deal with employees who spent a significant part of the workday at their desks attending to things other than work. Bob knew this was a universal conundrum. He'd read that three out of four employees take care of personal business at work, and that half of this group spend an average hour and twenty minutes a day doing so. [2] Well, Bob could personally relate. After all, how was a working guy supposed to order his wife's Valentine's Day roses or schedule car maintenance appointments, if not from the office? Obviously, though, much more could be accomplished at work if extracurricular chores could be handled in some other fashion.

Happily, once flexibility arrived, they were. No special directives or snippy memos were instrumental in the change, either. Amazingly enough, employees who were able to meet outside-of-work needs outside of work no longer felt compelled to do so on company time.

It was astonishing, Bob noticed, what giving people choices and allowing them a substantial degree of self-determination could accomplish. Suddenly, the people who worked for him felt more trusted and more respected. And their consequent actions served to further that trust and respect. With flexibility, absenteeism was dramatically reduced, project deadlines were met more consistently, and work quality significantly improved. Onerous, pointless meetings were replaced by productive ad hoc brainstorming sessions. Even office politics were no longer a hotbed of intrigue, since these highly focused flexible employees had little patience for them.

As Manager Bob soon realized, it was infinitely easier to manage a group of refreshed, focused, happy, loyal and grateful employees than a disgruntled, thinly-stretched, nap-craving band of early-retirement wannabees. And this definitely made Bob grin.

Bottom-line blessings

Hold on a minute, we suspect you are saying. Okay, so flexibility will make the work arena a kinder, gentler place. Great, it will make my job easier. But that in itself won't mean much unless my company is prospering. There must be bottom-line justification — and lots of it — for going so far as to end work as we know it.

We can't emphasize too strongly something mentioned elsewhere in this book (and something sure to be mentioned again). Introducing flexibility into an organization is a sound, savvy business decision. It is not an accommodation to employee needs. Flexibility, for all the satisfaction it brings to employees, is not a favor. It is a highly efficient, easily implemented, cost-effective and results-oriented competitive business strategy.

Needless to say, people who work for organizations must satisfy organizational demands. When Manager Bob meets the goals and objectives set for his process or department, his budget increases, his opportunities multiply, and his personal compensation reflects his achievements. Moreover, Bob's success allows those atop Bob in the corporate hierarchy to meet their own objectives, thus solidifying organizational success.

Flexibility helps Bob fulfill his goals and objectives and deliver against his budget. And it does so because giving employees options means giving Bob options, as well.

Let us give you an example. One of our longtime clients, an early convert to flexibility, is a large national marketing and strategic-planning firm. This firm employs numerous people, including copywriters, designers, researchers and account executives, in permanent part-time positions and in job shares. When a client comes on board, management assigns a team to meet that client's needs. The team consists of people with varying schedules, but the overlap between their schedules assures the client of full-time coverage, plus. By "plus" we mean there is virtually never any downtime because the client's sole contact is on a business trip, on vacation, or "in a meeting."

Now let's say this client decides, for economic reasons, to scale back their program for a time. Management does not have to let valuable talent go only to engage in expensive recruiting at some later date when the economy rebounds. Instead, employees are presented with options, reassigned as needed, and kept on board in a manner that suits them. Once the client is ready to ramp up, there is no learning curve to endure. Productivity is perfectly tailored to meet demand at virtually any point along the economic curve.

As part of this no-downtime strategy, flexibility allows Bob and other managers the latitude to move multi-talented employees from job to job. (A fact our research supports is that many employees will happily accept lateral moves in exchange for flexibility.) The enthusiasm with which new responsibilities are tackled counters employee boredom and burnout, generating even greater efficiency. When employees are allowed to show their stuff via new opportunities, half-hearted performances are never an issue.

Flexibility also helps Bob hold on to talent, in that it empowers him to engage in preemptive retention. Preemptive retention is just what it sounds like — it heads off attrition before it can begin. Our research shows that the mere possibility of flexibility in the offing discourages valued employees from looking for new jobs, because they know that these options will likely be available should they ever need to make use of them. (On the other hand, if flexible options don't exist at their workplace, they may walk out the door rather than try to be trailblazers.) So when Manager Bob receives a wedding invitation from one of his 28-year-old MBAs, he knows he can don his tux and enjoy the nuptial festivities without worrying how on earth he'll replace the bride or groom if they leave to start a family. (Yes, groom. Nowadays, more men than women say they would give up money to spend more time with their children. 3)

The upshot is that flexibility has gained Manager Bob a means of improving morale, productivity and retention — not to mention a better shot at meeting his numbers, whatever the prevailing economic conditions. But here's the best part: All of this costs Bob very little in terms of actual dollars spent. Flexibility can be implemented without great expense; moreover, it can be kept on the table as an employee incentive no matter what else needs to be removed.

Sure, when the good times roll it is considered *de rigueur* to hand out hefty bonuses and substantial salary increases, not to mention sweetening the incentive pot with lavish perquisites (pet insurance and at-desk massages, anyone?). But, as we know only too well, the good times are never uninterrupted. When things shift downward, tighter reins are kept on company cars and stock options lose their luster. Flexibility, on the other hand, actually looks better than ever.

Daily realities

If this sounds too easy, and you are suspicious as a result, relax. We don't mean to indicate that Manager Bob or any other manager can simply say, "Okay, let's be flexible," and then sit back and reap big rewards. Although flexibility is not a dollar-drainer, we all know there is no such thing as a truly free lunch. A commitment to flexibility must be just that — a commitment. Like all commitments, it must be backed up by meaningful and substantial action.

If managers are going to maximize the potential of their flexible employees, they must support those employees by committing to three key principles: sensible scheduling, sane supervision and continual communication.

By <u>sensible scheduling</u> we mean that managers must ensure that the times when the flexible worker will be working on site, working off site, or not working at all, meet the practical needs of both the employee and any team that the employee is a part of. This may be a simple task, or a more complex one, depending on several elements.

First, you'll need to ascertain and evaluate employee preferences (to be at home when the kids come in from school, for example, or take Thursdays off to drive their mother to physical therapy). Then you'll need to weigh their preferences against the cycle of weekly, monthly or quarterly departmental deadlines, relevant seasonal cycles (e.g. tax season at accounting firms or heat wave season at power companies), as well as customer expectations.

Just as important, you will need to use your people skills to match specific flexible options — permanent part time, telecommuting, job-sharing, phased retirement — with suitable personality styles. Is a particular worker a true self-starter who likes to work with a high degree of autonomy? Then telecommuting should suit them fine, whereas job-sharing might present an insurmountable challenge.

If your relationship with an employee is relatively new, you may not be able to make this judgement call right away. Alternatively, you may want to encourage them to engage in some frank self-evaluation or conduct a 360-degree assessment by their peers. Last but not least, you may simply need to accept that such things often require a period of trial and error. Set an agreement with the employee that includes a try-out period, and put well-defined criteria for the success of that period in place.

Our second principle, <u>sane supervision</u>, means that managers of flexible employees will need to implement procedures which value results more than face-time. In a nutshell, this translates into a single overriding practical strategy: no micromanaging.

Micromanaging any employee, in our experience, is not only a phenomenal waste of time but counterproductive in the sense that it makes employees feel untrustworthy and discourages their personal initiative. Micromanaging also fosters over-dependency — as in "my manager will fix it" — and even encourages outright lethargy. (As one refugee from a micro-managed situation told us, "I couldn't rouse myself to put much effort into a project when I knew no matter what I did, it would be redone.")

Even to attempt the micro-management of flexibly scheduled employees is beyond non-productive. It is antithetical to the positive nature of flexibility itself and would, quite frankly, be its death knell. There is little point in empowering and motivating employees with one hand while disempowering and second-guessing them with the other.

No matter how well-meaning your intentions may be, wise managers should resist the urge to hover over their flexible employees. Employees are grownups who know what they want and what they are capable of. And managers have better things to do with their time.

Attempts to have flexible employees report the completion of every task, or clue you in on the precise details of their days and weeks far in advance, will not advance your objectives. However, you sould still establish objectives, note important deadlines and put procedures in place for mutual updating. Flexible employees don't enjoy "being hung out to dry" any more than they appreciate being managerially mother-henned. The key to sane supervision of flexible employees is pretty much the same as the key to applying a measure of sanity to most anything — moderation.

What standard should you hold flexible employees to in the new work culture? The same as before: results. Too much wasted work time — whether wasted by traditionally scheduled employees looking busy while shopping online or by at-home employees watching *Live With Regis* — will ultimately reflect itself in poor performance and less overall output. As a manager, you will have to address these problems, and the employee who enjoys being employed must resolve them to your satisfaction. But flexible employees, in our experience, are less likely than others to ever put you in the position of calling them to account.

Before we leave the subject, one more aspect of sane supervision is simply not to treat employees that have alternative work arrangements as if they were second-class citizens. Of course, we appreciate that most managers would neither manifest such attitudes overtly nor hold them consciously. However, in our surveys, just over a quarter of flexibly employed respondents said their immediate supervisors treated them differently. Further elaboration regarding the difference in treatment by supervisors ranged from "not considered part of the company or team," to "not included in decisions and certain communications," to "viewed as less important."

Needless to say, employees cannot live up to their full potential if they feel ignored or disrespected. As for relegating flexible employees to more mundane or lower-priority work, it is wrongheaded to imagine that flexible employees will not be capable of or inclined to tackle more complex and fully integrated duties.

Finally, we come to our third essential tenet of managing flexible employees: <u>continual communication</u>. Note that we call this continual communication, as opposed to continuous communication. What's the difference? Continual refers to a steady repetition, over and over again. Continuous means unbroken and uninterrupted. What you want to do is put systems in place for regular communication with flexible employees. What you don't want is to make unreasonable demands or have expectations that these employees will continuously be available. Not only does the latter policy smack suspiciously of micromanaging but it will defeat the goal of flexible employees to reclaim some portion of their lives, and may instead lead to the burnout many of them are trying to avoid.

Nevertheless, continual communication is critical and you will need to come up with creative ways of making it happen. One consequence of flexibility (and a happy one, we assure you) is that you and your staff members will be conducting far fewer meetings. Meetings, in our experience — and in the opinion of an overwhelming majority of managers and employees we've polled — are often purposeless time-sucks that eat up large portions of the workday while providing needless opportunities for grandstanding, finger-pointing and other political pursuits. We believe you should rejoice in their diminishment. At the same time you will need to establish regular routines and means by which flexible employees can get information to and from colleagues, and address relevant work-related questions, issues and concerns with you.

It is not enough to instruct a flexible employee to "check in often." For one thing, people are bound to differ as to what "often" means. For another, everyone collaborating on a project must be able to make contact at pre-appointed times so that vital information doesn't slip through the cracks and critical decisions don't go unmade. What's required is an agreed-upon list of times when a flexible employee who is out of the office will check in or respond to e-mail and voicemail. In addition, if deemed useful, weekly times can be set for conference calls between all team members — including you, when appropriate.

Naturally, any plan should include contingencies for genuine emergencies. But we strongly urge you to use them only when truly necessary. In our experience, flexible workers rapidly become exceptionally skilled at the art of prioritization. They will know full well when they need to take advantage of extracurricular communications, and will do so unhesitatingly. However, they won't appreciate a manager who cries wolf and deems every issue, no matter how minor, a three-alarm emergency — any more than you would appreciate an employee who knocked on your door every time a matter required the slightest exercise in judgment.

Bringing flexibility out of the closet

By implementing sensible scheduling, sane supervision and continual communication, a manager will become an effective facilitator of flexible employment. However, in the long run, something more is necessary. To mine the true potential of flexibility, managers must become flexibility's champions.

As we write this, we are aware that some organizations endorse flexibility with little more than a wink and a nod. Ask someone at the top of these corporate hierarchies whether their company endorses alternative work arrangements and most will mumble a vague something-or-other about "deferring to the hiring manager." Such nebulous attitudes are better than overt repudiations. But while they beat a poke in the eye with a sharp stick, they do so only marginally. On behalf of the best interests of the company, of their departments, and of the employees who report to them, managers need to push for the formalization of flexible policies that have heretofore been "in the closet."

Why? Because formalization will allow a company to openly <u>assess</u> employee needs and preferences, to <u>market</u> their flexible polices, to <u>implement</u> flexible policies according to company-wide standards, and to objectively <u>evaluate</u> flexibility. Each of these abilities will greatly contribute to an organization's overall success.

<u>Assessment</u>, which can be conducted by any number of methods — including employee focus groups, surveys and one-on-one interviews — will do more than provide a company with solid information about what

employees want. It will also save substantial resources by preventing funds from being allocated to programs that employees actually don't want. A case in point: Our most recent survey, conducted in the Summer of 2001, clearly illustrates something many companies might find surprising. That is, 65 percent of our respondents deemed on-site childcare the least appealing of possible employee assistance programs. On the other hand, 57 percent deemed flexible work arrangements more important than salary, bonuses or stock options. Imagine how many misspent dollars companies might save if they only knew how their employee populations felt about these matters.

The marketing of flexible policies can also provide great benefit to companies. After all, how good is any good thing if it is kept a secret from those who value it? Getting the word out that a company endorses and promotes flexibility will help it attract top talent — whether straight from college or business school, from the existing workforce, or from those looking to return to it. Moreover, continual in-house marketing will alert (and later remind) employees of the various options that are available to them. The result: increased loyalty, even from those who may not wish flexibility in the short run. When one's options are open, one keeps an open mind about the future.

Implementing flexibility according to universal company standards will also help all parties involved. Clear written policies decrease ambiguity and provide objective reference points when questions regarding the specifics of flexibility arise. They also make all employees — including childless ones — feel included. Such policies — covering anything and everything from prorated salary and benefit plans to communication and home-office guidelines — need not be engraved in stone, of course. Extenuating circumstances are as wont to arise with regard to flexibility issues as they are to all things (life being no simple matter, after all). But intelligent exceptions to rules can never be made unless the rules themselves are intelligently defined.

Finally, openness about flexibility will enable objective <u>evaluation</u> of an organization's programs. Feedback can be solicited using methods similar to those used in initial-needs assessments (focus groups, surveys, one-on-one interviews), and cost-benefit analyses can be conducted on an ongoing basis.

<u>Evaluation</u> also allows for adjustments to policies and procedures, keeping them in sync with evolving circumstances. Moreover, the continual solicitation of input and feedback from flexible employees will prevent them from feeling as if they have second-class citizenship status within the company. In addition, flexible employees who fear (as our surveys show some 20 percent do) that their arrangements may keep them from future career advancement will have a chance to voice their concerns and thus influence company policies that might impact them.

Forging an HR alliance

Managers can bring assessment, marketing, standardized implementation and assessment into being by communicating honestly with HR about how flexibility works in their department. Yet, we realize that many managers are reluctant to interface with HR about flexibility. Some dread interference in informal arrangements that seem to be chugging along smoothly enough on their own. Others fear that clueing in HR might put an end to flexibility altogether, as the whole concept gets batted around the seemingly endless layers of the upper adminisphere.

In reality, managers bold enough to come forward about how flexibility is helping their departments (and more and more managers are doing so) generally find a high level of acceptance. In our experience, today's human resources personnel are extremely open to innovation in general and flexibility in particular. Their input can be an invaluable asset, and their stamp of approval a saving grace for any manager converted to — or even considering — alternative work arrangements.

Will there be resistance? Probably, as there is usually at least some resistance to anything new. It may be relatively short-lived, though, once potential benefits are objectively considered. However, the well-prepared manager should be ready for the most common objection to flexibility — the protestation that "if we give it to some people, everyone will want it."

The plain truth is that this is a fallacy. As much as we tout the advantages of flexibility, the world is comprised of all sorts of people with all kinds of agendas. Not everyone will be interested in flexibility, because for individual reasons — be they psychological, financial or logistical — flexibility simply isn't the right course for them. Indeed, contrary to initial expectations, many of our large clients have found that flexible jobs posted in-house may go unfilled as employees themselves demonstrate resistance to the new and untried.

In any event, this objection can be effectively countered by suggesting that HR institute a limited pilot program and study its effects. We fearlessly predict the pilot program will be so successful that instead of increasing the fear that "everyone will want flexibility," it will lead to the question: "How can we expand our flexible options?"

It's a good question — and one we will address at greater length in our next chapter.

8

The Job Share: Managing the Teamwork Ideal

Like most managers intrigued by the advantages that flexibility makes possible, you may be wondering what to do about positions that require full-time coverage. Should you simply resign yourself to relegating these jobs to employees with conventional schedules? If so, you will do your company a disservice. Demand for flexible work arrangements — and the many advantages they bring to an organization — will only increase in the years ahead. Why exclude a significant portion of your company's available employment?

Happily, there is a flexible solution that matches flexibly scheduled employees with full-time positions: the job share.

One of the most dynamic and success-generating flexible work arrangements (and, contrary to popular belief, one of the easiest to implement), the job share effectively distributes the responsibilities of a single, full-time position between two permanent part-time employees.

As it stands today, however, job-sharing is a woefully underutilized option in the American workplace. While it is true that, at the turn of the millennium, 22 percent of U.S. companies offered some type of job-share arrangement — the figure approached 59 percent among companies with 5,000 or more employees [1] — most only offered them on a small scale. The few that have been implemented often represent limited attempts to retain working mothers who return from maternity leave with a desire to cut back on their hours.

We believe the reasons for this underutilization are fear and confusion. Although human resources departments tend to embrace job-sharing, many middle managers are skeptical; they also view the creation and over-seeing of share teams as more difficult than it actually is. In this chapter, we aim to turn skeptics into supporters.

To that end, we'd like to make a couple of critical points right off the bat. First, designing and managing a job share is no different from operating any department successfully. In both instances, responsibilities are divided and employees are cognizant of one another's projects, covering for each other when the situation warrants it. Most important, they all communicate and contribute to the goals of the organization. Think of job-sharing as a microcosm of this dynamic, and your job-share management style will evolve naturally from there.

Second, most people's perception of what it means to "share" a job is skewed, since the basic concept of job-sharing is generally restricted to one rudimentary type — the equal skill-set job share, in which two people with similar abilities and experience split a workload more or less down the middle. We'll have more to say about other kinds of job shares later, but for now suffice to say that success with job-sharing, as with anything else, benefits from outside the box thinking. We have created several new and innovative types of shares that break the equal skill-set mold and liberate managers from its constraints while upping productivity and organizational well-being. We encourage you to keep an open mind about the kinds of teams you create, and the kinds of people you match up as share partners.

Before elaborating, we want to mention a few of the many benefits that job-sharing can bring to your department and your company.

A wealth of benefits

When it comes to job-sharing, less is more. By this we mean that having two people each work fewer hours will result in <u>improved and extended coverage</u> for virtually any position.

If your organization is like most, there are undoubtedly jobs that seem to demand more than any one individual — no matter how competent and dedicated — can possibly keep up with. These run the gamut from administrative assistant to the company comptroller. In-between might be a copywriter, an engineer, a product manager, or an account executive for a demanding client. Wouldn't it be wonderful if these jobs could have someone working at them, say, six days a week — with virtually no down-time lost to vacation?

With job-sharing, this kind of set-up is eminently possible. All that's needed are two permanent part-time employees working three days a week (e.g. Monday, Tuesday and Wednesday for Employee A and Wednesday, Thursday and Friday for Employee B). Employees A and B can also arrange their schedules so that they never take the same vacation week. (Generally this is no great hardship for anyone who is working on a flexible schedule to begin with.) The result is a guaranteed 52 weeks of coverage a year for you and your clients. As certain industries make the transition to a 24/7 model, job-share schedules can also be arranged to suit specific organizational needs while still suiting the needs of employees.

With job-sharing, in fact, positions that formerly placed unrealistic, stress-inducing demands on a single employee no longer require superhuman feats from potential heart-attack candidates. Instead, these positions can be manned by a pair of sane, well-rested teammates who show up raring to go, thanks to reinvigorating downtime and a fresh perspective.

What about <u>continuity</u>, you ask? It's still solidly there — not just as a result of "overlap Wednesday" face-time, but because of team communication strategies that you, as manager of a job-share team, helped put in place (more about this later). Continuity is also there, in the sense that should one job-share team member leave, the other can not only soldier on but quickly bring a new partner up to speed.

While on the subject, we'll add that employee turnover is apt to be far less of a problem with job-share team members than with regular full-time employees. The burnout factor is lower and the incentive to stay is greater. Job-sharers tell us that even if their life circumstances were altered in some significant way, their work arrangements are such that they would try to stay on with their employer. They want to stay because they are content and, hence, their *commitment* is strong.

Recruiting advantages are another benefit of job-sharing programs. Because job-sharing allows employees to work reduced hours without sacrificing fulfilling, challenging work at their level, these programs serve to attract highly desirable employees to companies that are wise enough to market them. They also allow these organizations to tap into what we have come to call the Great Untapped Brain Trust that exists in the workplace today.

We regularly encounter candidates who tell us sad tales of having "dumbed down" their resumes in order to find a job that will offer them a chance to work less than the traditional 40-hour week. We know comptrollers who have presented themselves as bookkeepers, public relations directors who downwardly morphed into "publicists," and former vice presidents who, upon reentering the workforce after taking time off to raise a family, reincarnated as "associate directors." Many of them follow the practice of a candidate who explained: "I left the last three jobs off my resume altogether. I obliterated seven years of my life, during which I had gone from being an assistant manager of a small customer-service department to running a 225-person operation for a large manufacturer. I thought that in order to work part time, I might just have to go back to working the phones."

Happily, this job seeker found a position commensurate with her skills because of a new job-sharing policy implemented by another large consumer products manufacturing firm. What some employers already know

— and many more are about to learn — is that there is an abundance of unmined talent that consists of people who are selling themselves short just to obtain a manageable work/life balance. Job-sharing offers such individuals a dignified reentry into the workforce, and it offers the companies that hire them a tremendous ROI for dollars spent on the promotion of job-sharing initiatives.

We can't leave the subject without pointing out the undeniable veracity of an old adage: Two heads are, indeed, better than one. A job-share team provides its employer with access to two sets of experiences, two sets of talents and two sets of ideas. The result is a unique kind of creative thinking that, in effect, renders the whole of each team greater than the sum of its parts.

Creating top teams is simpler than you think

One might suspect that once the benefits of job-sharing are explored, most companies would implement a job-share program immediately. Alas, this is often not the case. Again, we think resistance to job-sharing manifests to a large degree because managers imagine that this form of flexible employment is more difficult to put in place than other flexible options such as telecommuting or permanent part time.

Obviously one isn't simply going to wander around the office saying, "Okay, you and, um, you there — let's have you share a job." That, of course, is not the way a good manager puts together *any* team of employees, be they full time or otherwise. Time and thoughtful consideration are always well spent in creating a mix of co-workers who will thrive by working in tandem and who exhibit the personality traits, work habits and work ethics appropriate to an organization's culture. You will need to rely on these standard guidelines when matching share teams.

What you need not do, however, is to feel apprehensive that job-sharing will require you to match up duos consisting of virtual employee "clones."

The <u>equal skill-set share</u>, in which partners have relatively the same amount of experience and the same fundamental responsibilities, is only one type of job share. Even in this type of arrangement, however, it is best to match two people whose temperaments and strong suits complement rather than replicate each other's. An introspective, detail-oriented person and an outgoing, big-picture-strategizing work-mate can — and do — attack a project from two different yet correlating perspectives.

Besides, as we've said, although the equal skill-set team represents the conventional concept of job-sharing, it is far from the only option. We looked closely at departments and teams where people work well in concert to get the job done and discovered that most employees are already sharing jobs in some way with one or more of their colleagues, regardless of who works what hours. Based on this practical reality, we came up with new models for job-sharing that are often even more useful than the simple equal skill-set version.

One of the most practical job shares is the <u>complementary skill-set share</u>, in which each member of a two-person team offers skills and experience in certain areas where the other partner is comparatively weak. This type of job share probably already exists in your company today — between full-time workers.

An example of this type of job share was implemented ad hoc by two men we know — both full-time employees — who shared the title of co-vice president of product development for a major kitchenware manufacturer. One excelled in design aesthetics, while the other focused on technical engineering. The former, a "people person," enjoyed handling the personnel responsibilities that went into managing a 75-person department; the latter loved to crunch numbers and handled forecasting. Together, they created an ideal package.

And here's another interesting aspect of this arrangement: It also ended up as a <u>geographic job share</u>, with the first team member remaining at the company's East Coast headquarters while the second relocated to a

Western city that housed a major company plant. Together they covered multiple time zones with great efficiency.

Another type of job share that already exists between full-timers, and one growing in popularity, is the <u>mentor-subordinate share</u>. Here, a very experienced employee teams up with a less experienced but promising subordinate. Each handles the tasks commensurate with his or her skill level and experience. The more experienced member can orchestrate the big picture and deal with complex situations and tough clients. The subordinate can handle the more routine aspects of the job, learning all the while. In the best-case scenario, the subordinate is mentored to take over the position when the superior is promoted. This type of share is highly cost-effective in two ways: First, because each team member is paid according to his level; second, because the company is able to promote from within rather than engaging in an expensive recruiting process.

The chemistry of job shares

As with any position, staffing a job share involves defining what needs to be done and then figuring out who can do it best. Is "people-chemistry" important? Sure, the same way it is when you staff any departmental position.

Unless you're in the market to hire a lighthouse keeper or a cave-dwelling monk, all jobs involve people skills and all good employees know how to successfully negotiate relationships with co-workers. A manager can increase the likelihood of good people-chemistry by teaming co-workers whose personalities and habits, while not identical, mesh well.

In some cases, job-share applicants will pre-select their own partners and approach management with what we call a "two-headed resume," along with a proposal for just how the job share will function. If this happens, you already have a leg up.

The team that applies for a job together has put a great deal of time, effort and thought into crafting their plan. Moreover, the mere fact that they have successfully completed their first project — a joint resume and proposal — is an excellent portent and bodes well for their future collaborative efforts. Of course, as a manager you will need to ask the same kind of smart questions you would of any job applicant, and also ensure that both potential team members understand their roles and responsibilities. You should set goals with the team and implement a trial period during which you can see if these are being met; then, if necessary, refine procedures.

In some cases, you may need to fill half of a job share, matching a new partner with an employee whose old partner has left. In others, you may need to locate a suitable match for a valued employee who is cutting back to permanent part time. Or, as in an increasing number of instances, you might decide to staff a position as a job share from the start — in which case, you will need to recruit and match two new employees.

Again, as with any potential new hires, you will need to check specific experience and qualifications. You will also want to learn up front a fair amount with regard to the personalities of the candidates. An applicant's references should offer insight into whether the person under consideration takes the term "team player" seriously, is willing to share information — and credit — with a fellow employee, or is wont to engage in territoriality. (One thing you definitely don't want in any position, let alone a job-share, is someone who *won't* share.)

If your human resources department routinely administers a simple personality inventory, such as the Myers Briggs Type Indicator (MBTI)[2], you should use the information it yields. Implemented by a number of major companies for screening job applicants, the MBTI consists of a series of two-choice items that concern personal preferences and inclinations, with results yielding 16 possible personality types. The test, for which interpretative materials are available, is particularly useful in pointing out tendencies such as introversion versus extroversion; it can also indicate how someone gathers information, makes decisions and relates to others.

Whatever information *you* gather must be supplemented by your own intuition. Listen carefully to how job candidates respond to your questions and trust your gut to send you a warning if they strike you as "off." What are a candidate's goals? Are they similar to the goals of his or her potential partner? They should be. What about work style? Do they like to plan ahead or do they perform best when up against a deadline? Could they tolerate working with someone whose style is different from, but compatible with, their own? Do they consider themselves flexible? Can they give you an example of a new situation where they successfully adapted?

Pick up on cues and clues as you process the answers you receive. Notice, for example, if an applicant seems willing to share the limelight when talking about past accomplishments. Are they in the habit if saying "we" or is it always "I, I, I"?

This may sound like a lot of effort, but we assure you it doesn't require any more diligence than any sound hiring process — and the payoff is substantial. Moreover, the best news about filling a position with a job-share team is that you don't need just one candidate to fill all the qualifications on your wish list. The blended talents of two individuals are much more likely to provide the perfect package.

Fostering communications

Once your job-share team is in place, your role as manager will involve outlining expectations, defining roles and responsibilities, setting goals, and discussing the means for reaching these goals. In addition, you should foster best practices for effective communication between job-share team members (none of which is any different from effectively managing the rest of your employees.) Indeed, if we were asked to sum up the three most important aspects of a job-share or any effective team, we would have to say communication, communication and communication.

All workplace relationships need to accommodate differences and difficulties. The teams that best weather work's demands are those with a forum for talking things through, listening respectfully, and tolerating — even capitalizing on — aspects of their co-workers that differ from their own. Such colleagues not only tend to function best on a day-to-day basis, but will also soldier on in the face of high pressure, even crisis, because they have a relationship built on forthrightness and the trust it engenders.

If you want a job-share team that functions brilliantly as a unit, help them understand that the commitment to communication is vital. Empower them to put in place communication practices that are consistent and reliable. Ask them to spell out in writing what their communication protocols will be. How often, and via what means, will they interact with each other, with you, with other department members, and with clients? Be sure to determine how they will document these communications, so that each job-share partner can follow a logical trail to see exactly what the other has done.

No micromanaging

We recommend tackling logistical issues up front, including whether there will be beginning-of-the-day and/or end-of-the-day check-in calls, and if it's practical for the team to share an e-mail address and a single computer password. Decide if there will always be an overlap day, or if there will be any time when both team members are out of the office simultaneously.

After you offer your expertise and encouragement, be sure to step back and allow the team room to work out any kinks that may arise. We don't suggest micromanaging job-share teams any more than you would your other employees. There's nothing to be gained by hovering over a team and obsessing about minutiae. If you have chosen your team members wisely, they will surely develop a near-seamless system in short order, refining it as they go along. If there is a fundamental flaw, it will show up soon enough — without your having to do anything to unearth it.

Evaluating and compensating the job-share team

Let's spend some time here on the topics of evaluation and compensation. Managers often express some degree of confusion about these matters. Again, they are relatively simple to deal with if you already have sound routine guidelines in place.

With regard to evaluation, a job-share team should be reviewed as a unit. Look at the position virtually the same way you would if it were covered by one employee. Are the goals of the position being met? Is initiative being shown? Is dedication evident? And, of course, how have the results manifested themselves? These questions are no different from the ones you would ask when evaluating the performance of a single employee. Again, job-sharing does not add to your workload. It does, however, distribute the workload more efficiently, and with more far-reaching results. But we know what you're thinking. Shouldn't you assess whether both members of the team are pulling their weight? Actually, you won't need to. Chances are high, if part one of your evaluation has come up positive, they are. On the other hand, if there were a problem, you would have heard about it. It's true that some job-share teams don't work out, usually for the same reason other employees might not — bad chemistry. However, there's no need to throw out the entire job-sharing system, any more than you would blame the normal work schedule when a conventionally employed professional failed to perform effectively.

As for compensation, in general the key here is prorating. Typically, a flexibly scheduled employee is compensated, in both time and benefits, based on what percentage of a "full-time" schedule they work. Hence, if they work three days a week, they receive 60 percent of what a full-time employee would receive for performing the same job. Following this logic, members of an <u>equal skill-set</u> job share, in which partners have similar experience and areas of expertise, and a <u>complementary skill-set</u> job share, in which equally talented partners handle different aspects of the same responsibilities, should also be compensated on a prorated basis depending on their schedules.

But these are by no means difficult to configure. Members of a <u>mentor-subordinate</u> job share would be compensated, on a prorated basis, for the level of job they hold. As for geographic job shares, your HR department will need to advise you if salary guidelines vary according to the cost of living in different regions.

A firsthand endorsement

We hope that by now we have alleviated many of the reservations you may have held about job-sharing as a staffing strategy that is good for companies, good for employees and good for you as a manager. If not, consider this: We are living proof of the success of job-sharing, for we have run our company as a job share since day one — and have accrued all of its many benefits.

With each of us spending certain days in the office, including some overlap time, we have achieved better-than-full-time coverage. Alike in our goals, but different in our way of accomplishing them, we cheerfully defer to our partner when she is better at doing some particular task. Our communication is fluid and complete, and we have developed the kind of mental shorthand that allows us to easily finish each other's sentences. We share triumphs and disappointments, though there have been far more of the former than the latter, largely because of the way we have organized our joint responsibilities and balanced our lives in the process.

From a business perspective, our greatest achievement is how well we have managed to leverage our flexible staffing model in service of our clients. After all, without satisfying the customer, the rest wouldn't matter much. And customer satisfaction is what our next chapter is all about.

9

Why the Customer Wins

In the last two chapters, we discussed the advantages that flexibility brings to employees, employers and managers alike. Yet we are aware that these advantages would add up to very little real benefit if it were not for one final factor in the equation: the customer. After all, unless a business effectively meets the needs of its customers, it won't be providing much employment at all — flexible or otherwise.

We know for a fact that employers who embrace flexibility service their customers exceptionally well. In all our years of experience, we have never heard a client complaint with regard to flexibly scheduled employees. Not one. Moreover, our surveys clearly and consistently indicate that flexibly scheduled employees are not only meeting but also exceeding the expectations of their organizations' customers.

Why is this customer smiling?

Once again, we'll refer to the hypothetical example of Rip Van Worker, with which this book began. As you'll recall, the profits of the company that had instituted flexible policies were up; meanwhile, the company's competition — which had eschewed flexible employment — had failed. We firmly believe this will be exactly what happens in the actual non-hypothetical future. Customer satisfaction will take a noticeable upturn, and flexibility will become a cornerstone of successful customer-relationship management.

We'll take a moment here to enumerate the many benefits that customers will enjoy when the companies they get their products and services from are staffed by a significant percentage of flexible employees.

There will be more "up" time. One of our regular accounts is a large marketing firm with an extensive roster of Fortune 500 clients. To handle some of its key accounts, this firm routinely puts together staffs of five or six flexibly scheduled employees that together provide greater coverage over longer hours than a conventional staff could. Under traditional staffing, one person is usually responsible for client relations (for example, an account executive at an advertising or PR agency). But when they're sick or on vacation, the client is no longer served at the highest level. In fact, in an effort to "always be available to the client," account managers must work extraordinary hours, making themselves available even during vacations, a situation that often leads to burnout. In the flexible scenarios we have introduced to account teams, however, there is always more than one person to handle client relations, which ensures that the client feels better "cared for" and that members of the team feel less burdened.

What's more, with a flexible team at their disposal, clients are rarely left dangling due to employee vacations, illness, business travel, and the like, because someone on the team is nearly always available to meet their needs.

Higher energy levels will prevail. In addition to having someone available all the time, clients who work with teams of flexible employees find that their contacts have more to offer in terms of energy and enthusiasm. As one explained, "There are fewer brain belches overall. When people have time to refuel, they are more on the ball."

There will be more productivity in each billable hour. Clients that work with flexibly scheduled employees, simply put, get more bang for their buck. These employees are far less likely to indulge in extracurricular matters while at work, which means that customers won't be funding the average hour and 20 minutes a day that the typical full-time employee spends booking doctor appointments, holding the line at Motor Vehicles, or lining up babysitters.

They will work with a higher caliber of employee. Remember that there
is a Great Untapped Brain Trust out there. Eminently qualified individuals will return to the work force in droves once they are aware they can
secure challenging, meaningful employment, at their level, on a part-time
basis. This Untapped Brain Trust, which consists of everyone from MBA
moms returning to work to highly experienced retirees with a great deal of
value to contribute, will raise the talent quotient of any organization, and
customers will benefit accordingly.

There will be greater creativity. Flexibility not only provides a more talented team, but a more creative one, as well. If two heads are better than
one, then five or six offer greater potential than two. Besides, creativity
tends to flourish in an environment where everyone comes to work with a
modicum of rest and relaxation under their belts.

Customers will reap the rewards of a lower turnover rate. Surely there is
not a customer in the world unfamiliar with the frustrations of having a
trusted account manager, sales representative or other key contact leave
their team at relatively short notice. When a replacement comes in —
often after much elapsed time when no one is minding the store, so to
speak — the learning curve must begin anew. It can be months before the
previous contact's replacement comes up to speed.

The good news is that this may never happen again if customers work
with flexibly scheduled employees, since fewer such employees will leave
their jobs. But if and when one does, there is likely someone else on the
team who is up to speed, and can step in and fill the void.

Customers will always have someone they can relate to. Offering a
wider variety of people with whom customers can interact increases the
likelihood that they will find someone to whom they relate well on a personal level. One of our clients is a Connecticut marketing and promotions
agency that employs more than 45 creative and account people, all part
time, for some of the biggest brand names in the U.S. Each agency team
has more than one "go-to" person — each with his or her own area of
expertise — who understands and can deliver the services necessary to

meet client needs. This, in effect, is an ideal "complementary skill set" — a job share in which professionals who have different areas of expertise work together to deliver a product or service better than they could alone.

In addition to these specific benefits, there is another advantage that, though more amorphous, is perhaps most significant of all. It's the underlying confidence that customers have in companies whose employees are content.

Offering employees the opportunity to balance work with the rest of their lives displays an attitude that is not only smart but also respectful and humane. It says a lot about your organizational culture and it communicates to the customer that you understand and embrace one of the primary rules of business today: If you don't treat your employees right, you can't service your customers right.

Honesty: the best and only policy

Treating employees well, of course, means more than allowing them to work in a flexible manner. It means offering direction that will help them succeed in doing their jobs and in meeting customers' expectations. To this end, anyone who manages flexible employees can also offer valuable guidance for maximizing customer satisfaction.

First and foremost, we suggest that organizations fully disclose all matters relating to the scheduling of staff with whom customers will be working. For their part, employees should be encouraged to be as clear and specific as possible with clients about when they are in the office, who will be handling their responsibilities when they are out, and when and how they can be reached by e-mail and phone. Not doing so is a recipe for disaster.

We know of an entrepreneur who was reluctant to tell the customers of her small graphic arts firm that most of her employees worked flexibly on various schedules, including part time and telecommuting. She had the idea (very much mistaken) that revealing this would somehow make her operation seem less professional. Her insecurity led her to encourage employees to be less than transparent about their individual working hours.

You probably won't be surprised to learn that this strategy backfired. Confused clients wondered why certain staffers stammered when asked if they could meet on Tuesday afternoon, and why others never seemed to answer their phones on Friday. Things fell through cracks because the staff was not working as a team but as many disparate entities — each trying to protect their "secret schedules." When this type of scenario arises, the predictable response is to say, "See, we tried to be flexible, but it failed." The policy gets the rap, but the problem was the dishonesty. Consider this: If a traditionally employed person misled a client, would you blame his work schedule?

In this case, enough complaints arose that company policy was altered. Staffers who were out of the office on Tuesdays were now free to say: "My colleague, so-and-so will be here on that day. He is completely up to date on your projects and will be happy to work with you." And those who telecommuted on Fridays were free to give out their home office phone numbers.

Not only did the clients feel better, so did the employees. No longer constrained by trying to obfuscate the truth, they banded together to make sure every project was covered by more than one person, that communication flowed freely, and that contingency plans were always in place. No one wanted to lose their flexibility, and the employees instinctively understood that the best way to maintain their flexible situation was to cooperate in providing the best possible service to their clients.

Employee accountability

What happened at that particular firm is indicative of dynamics everywhere when it comes to keeping customers happy. Organizational honesty is a critical factor. Employee accountability is another.

Flexible employees on the whole are a highly responsible group of people who relish the idea of being held accountable for their actions. They do not want to sneak around pretending to be something they're not. They are proud and pleased to be doing productive, creative work on a schedule that makes sense for them. Given a little encouragement, they will find amazingly resourceful ways to do what needs to be done during any specified period of time. In the spirit of enlightened self-interest, they will cooperate with one another so that, as far as customers are concerned, their schedules are seamless.

Flexible employees do not need, want or expect to be coddled. Indeed, they understand that any perception that they are being favored or "spoiled" will ultimately create a resentful backlash. To avoid this, they will appreciate a manager who preempts potential misunderstandings by asking them to demonstrate how they will meet customer needs from the moment the mere possibility of a flexible schedule is discussed. They will also appreciate a manager who challenges them to continually enhance and refine their performance, regardless of when and where they work.

We recently came across an intriguing article in *The Harvard Business Review*. It was based on a failed scenario of flexibility that resulted in tremendous employee backlash. The article correctly noted that managers often labor under the misapprehension that flexible schedules should be doled out as *Queen-for-a-Day*-type prizes to employees who can prove the greatest personal hardships imposed by a traditional full-time schedule. But as the article points out, this is a recipe for an office morale disaster and an undermining of the teamwork principle. Workplace benefits of any nature should be dispensed in recognition of jobs done well. [1] Flexibility, on the other hand, should be reserved for employees who can meet or exceed customer expectations. Flexibility needs to be a clearly stated policy available to everyone but contingent upon employees demonstrating how their workload will be carried out on a part-time basis.

Naturally, managers play a critical role in facilitating the ability of flexible employees to collectively succeed. Managers must make sure that the right technological tools are available, and they must ascertain what technology customers feel comfortable with, and under what circumstances. They must advocate that employees communicate consistently and effectively, not only with customers but also with one another — fostering an atmosphere of mutual respect and appreciation in which everyone is willing to go the extra mile. In such an environment there is simply no situation that cannot be handled efficiently and intelligently, as customers won't fail to notice.

Building a customer-pleasing team

Until now, we have primarily addressed how embracing flexibility will impact organizations that are already up and running on a largely conventional model. We want to point out as well that small and medium-size start-up companies, along with new spin-off divisions of large organizations, can utilize flexibility from the moment of inception to build a team of employees that is exceptionally responsive to the needs of customers.

After we founded Flexible Resources, Inc. we added each staff member to meet a particular customer-driven demand. We hired people to answer the phones when call volume was highest and when we needed to be off doing other things. We hired recruiters to interview candidates at locations that candidates found easily accessible. And we arranged job shares for staffers who interacted with corporate clients, basing these on factors that ranged from compatible geography and schedules, to behavioral-style attunement, to individual areas of expertise.

This strategy allowed us to provide our candidates and corporate clients alike with exceedingly responsive, personalized service. And it gave us other practical advantages, too, including the ability to grow at a manageable pace.

New businesses don't necessarily fail because their owners' ideas are bad. They tend to fail because their owners expand too quickly, take out too many loans and make staffing errors.

The biggest and most common staffing mistake lies in thinking that the top professionals they need are only available full time. In fact, conventional staffing is the least productive and most expensive way to meet a growing organization's staffing needs. It is a relic whose time has come...and gone. Flexibility, on the other hand, can help minimize an organization's growing pains.

For anyone attempting to build a nimble, scaleable, customer-responsive company, we strongly suggest doing it the flexible way. Flexibility will allow you to:

- let the customers' needs dictate the pace and scope of growth because you hire staff based on *their* needs;
- attract and effectively service geographically far-flung customers;
- control cash flow and overhead costs;
- make the most of a limited staffing budget;
- hire top talent that will remain enthusiastic and committed as your organization expands.

As we have already seen, a growing number of professionals are discovering the joys of working on a flexible schedule. Meanwhile, there are people starting new businesses, new departments and new divisions who need top-flight employees to help them attract and retain the loyal customers who will grow their organizations to the next level. Never has it been so simple to take advantage of such a perfect dynamic. Future success will lie with those who recognize this opportunity, and act on it.

10

Redefining Time: The Future of Flexibility

At one point in Franz Kafka's life, the author took a job at an insurance company in Prague. Writing to his girlfriend about his daily experiences, he commented, "I'm not complaining about the work so much as the swampy viscosity of time…You blame everything on your watch, which you hold constantly in the palm of your hand." [1]

How many of us who have worked for any sort of organization can relate to that feeling of angst? Virtually everyone, we're sure. And when we felt that way on the job, we knew something else: We were most assuredly not doing our best work — that is, if we were doing any work at all.

Time, and its effective use, has always posed a conundrum for business. Nearly a century ago, a man named Frederick Winslow Taylor, America's first organizational guru and the author of *The Principles of Scientific Management*, preached that there was one "best" and most efficient method of doing anything. His philosophy, the eponymous Taylorism, held that people needed to be told precisely how to do their jobs, and at what pace.

In a famous experiment at Bethlehem Steel, Taylor applied his scientific management principles to pig-iron handlers. These workers typically loaded just over 12 tons a day of 90-plus pounds of crude iron blocks (known as "pigs") onto railway cars. Selecting an energetic worker as a "case study," Taylor offered to increase the worker's wages from $1.15 to $1.85 per day if he followed prescribed procedures to increase his output. Soon this worker, known as the "little Dutchman," was loading 47.5 tons of pig iron a day. This must have been very gratifying indeed to his employer — especially since nearly everyone else quit.[2]

While we don't mean to mock the legitimate efforts of Taylor and others to standardize production, we don't know many people who could, would or should work the way the "little Dutchman" worked. Fortunately, much has changed since the time of Taylorism. Today, 90 percent of us work in white-collar jobs. Today, technology serves us, rather than we it. Most important of all, today we don't see organizations changing people so much as we see people changing organizations. But even though we have shifted from a manufacturing to a service economy, one thing hasn't changed — management's never-ending thirst to improve productivity.

In a service economy, judging productivity is trickier. After all, your financial analyst or senior brand manager isn't sitting at a desk all day producing widgets. But as more and more technological innovations are put at our disposal, managers feel entitled to demand more and better results from their staff of professionals.

In the spring of 2001, we surveyed more than 500 job seekers who were looking for flexible work arrangements. Additionally, we surveyed hundreds of professionals already working in flexible positions and dozens of managers at companies from small businesses on up to the Fortune 500 that employed at least some professionals on a flexible basis. Our findings, which largely speak for themselves, clearly show that flexibility continues to expand and thrive.

We believe, and we have the research to back it up, that there is no more effective management strategy for improving productivity at the professional level than flexible staffing. Simply put, non-traditional staffing strategies energize, motivate and focus employees in ways that are undeniable.

Consider:

- Two-thirds of our more than 500 candidates said they would be more productive in flexible jobs.
- 45 percent of those in flexible jobs said they <u>are</u> more productive.
- 75 percent of employers said their most recently hired flexible professional is "among the best" or "better than most" employees in the company.
- 45 percent of managers surveyed said their flexible employees are "more focused" than full-time staff working a conventional schedule.
- 32 percent said their flexible staff is "more motivated" than those working a traditional 9-to-5 schedule.
- 26 percent said their flexible staff is more "results-oriented."
- 59 percent of employers said flexibility is an important tool for attracting and retaining talent.

These are just a few of the eye-opening statistics that reveal the impact of non-traditional staffing on productivity. Now let's examine flexibility's more far-reaching implications, including its impact on our society and the way we are choosing to live our lives in the 21st century.

- 56 percent of our candidates in a flexible work arrangement report that they *never* plan to go back to traditional employment.
- 44 percent of our flexibly employed candidates see themselves as working in some sort of part-time arrangement for the rest of their lives rather than retiring permanently.
- The younger the professional, the more likely they are to request a flexible work schedule — and the more likely they are to quit if they don't get one.

And consider what the following statistics reveal about the seriousness and stability of the flexible professional.

- 27 percent of the candidates we have placed in flexible positions are the primary breadwinners in their households. An additional 26 percent are co-breadwinners, earning an amount equal to their partners' contributions. Clearly, flexible employment has evolved well beyond any point where it can be construed as jobs for mommy-trackers waiting for their young children to enter school. (*20 percent of all our candidates are childless*). Moreover, flexibility is definitely not for workplace dilettantes who are uncommitted to their careers. (*73 percent of our candidates believe that flexible employment will not harm their careers.*) Flexibly scheduled employees are supporting themselves and their families while performing vital functions both at home and in the workplace. It's also worth nothing that, between 1998 and 2000, the median personal income of our placed candidates rose from $48,000 to $62,000.

- Of all our candidates placed in temporary positions, 76 percent are on long-term projects of more than three months. 27 percent work full-time in flexible arrangements. As employers get their feet wet and try flexible arrangements, they are finding they like them — possibly more than they ever imagined.

- 34 percent of flexibly employed candidates are working in jobs that involve some telecommuting. Employers are increasingly more comfortable with telecommuting, and relinquishing their fears that far-flung employees will spend the day clipping their hedges. In fact, managers with flexible employees who telecommute say that telecommuters beat all other staff in terms of their ability to communicate with colleagues.

- 49 percent of the candidates we have placed are in <u>permanent</u> flexible jobs. We are not, in fact, becoming a nation of free agents, as some have speculated, so much as we are enjoying more freedom while retaining the security of remaining on the payroll. The permanent nature of so many flexible jobs reflects employees' commitment to progressive organizations, as well as the commitment of these organizations to valued employees.

In addition to facts and figures, we'd like to share a few telling quotes from people currently working in flexible positions.

"I find my part-time job to be just as or more rewarding than full time. I'm more focused, more motivated, and am learning more in this position than in former full-time positions."

"The level of responsibility and authority is greater than I expected."

"I am more motivated, experience less stress and spend less time commuting."

"This has been a great situation because the person I work for is very open to the idea and wants to give me challenges and keep me motivated. My boss appreciates the help now more than when I worked full time. Every minute counts more now, and nothing is taken for granted."

"This has improved both my work and my family balance."

"Management appreciates the role I play, and the support I give them."

"I realized how capable I am and how valuable my experience is."

"I value my productivity improvement. There are fewer meetings and more focus."

"I don't get caught up in office politics anymore."

"Management is so receptive. They respect my work and input."

"A large organization is accepting and promoting flexible arrangements. It's terrific!"

◆   ◆   ◆   ◆   ◆

Can we promise you that the workplace will become largely flexible tomorrow, next month or next year? No, but we can promise you that the end of work as we know it looms on the horizon.

The kind of critical mass necessary to inspire a complete paradigm shift is building. By the time teenagers entering high school today enter the workforce, the 9-to-5 mode will be one of many options — and not the most prevalent of popular ones, we assure you.

Foreseeing the future

When people hear us talk about flexibility and the end of work as we know it, they often ask "Won't that change many other things about the way we live?" Indeed it will. As you will recall from the beginning of this book, we believe that the adoption of flexible work schedules will ripple throughout society, causing a number of positive changes.

On an individual level, it will bring about such desirable effects as:

- children who spend more time in the care of at least one parent;
- healthier sleep patterns;
- less work-related stress and absenteeism.

On an organizational level, flexibility will lead to businesses that:

- adapt more readily to shifting economic conditions — and flourish under a wider variety of circumstances;
- are better able to serve customers globally;
- have a competitive advantage in attracting new talent and retaining the best professionals;
- enjoy expanded options for problem-solving.

Those willing to consider the vast array of non-traditional staffing options will open themselves to an infinite array of possibilities for setting up new departments and even starting new companies, by using their personnel more effectively. (For example, as cited in our chapter on job-sharing, often by teaming up professionals with complementary skills.) And by looking at candidates who seek flexibility, companies open themselves to a far greater talent pool than they might otherwise encounter. On the plus side of the ledger for society as a whole:

- We'll have more time to participate in family and community life, if we so choose.

- We'll have cleaner air and less reliance on fossil fuels because of dramatically reduced auto traffic.

- People won't be "put out to pasture" in their senior years but will continue to contribute throughout their lives.

So far, so good.

But we also foresee that the forthcoming paradigm shift will, like all major changes, require some serious readjustments. There are many social issues to confront and negotiate as we move toward a new way of working and living.

Inter-generation teamwork — Nearly 20 percent of American workers will be over 55 by the year 2015. [3] For most "Boomers" in the workplace, retirement will not occur all at once. Instead, it will be accomplished in phases of increasingly reduced flexible schedules. Boomers will stay active and involved while supplementing their pensions with earned income. Companies will reap the benefit of their experience.

Many major corporations, including PepsiCo, Lockheed Martin, Monsanto, and Avaya, are already offering phased retirement. Many more are expected to follow, with the passage of appropriate phased-retirement legislation (already on deck) that allows for the prorating of pension plans. [4]

What this will translate to, in terms of day-to-day reality, is an increased cooperative mentoring dynamic in the workplace. Older workers will share their knowledge freely with younger ones, and relinquish any fear they might have that they're hastening their own exits. Indeed, the better they are as mentors, the more they will be able to write their own tickets in terms of working when, where and how they want.

In turn, younger workers will come to value the skills and information that older workers can impart. Rather than viewing the over-50 crowd as a herd of dinosaurs (and gazing wistfully skyward for the meteor that will extinguish them), post-Boomer generations will need to respect what their elders have to offer.

But can we evolve our corporate culture from one that often seems to pit older and younger workers against each other into one where multiple generations exist in harmony? (The latter, after all, is the way humankind has prospered throughout most of history.) The answer is, we must. Ultimately, the best and the brightest among us will gravitate toward organizations that hold all generations in high esteem. It will not be lost on the young that they, too, will grow older and will wish to live and work well once they do.

Turnkey technology — There was a time not long ago when IT departments were isolated, self-contained entities within business organizations. Now, however, information technology is a critical aspect of any business transaction. Enterprise software links every process from sales and marketing, to production, to personnel, to finance. Network technology is flowing past organizational boundaries, connecting companies to customers, suppliers, service-providers and other partners around the globe.

Technophobes and Luddites take note: You no longer have an excuse for avoiding techno-literacy. A high comfort level with technology will soon be more than just an option for anyone who wants to work flexibly — or for anyone who wants to work at all.

Sure, we know IT doesn't always perform as advertised. But when it works the way it should, the results are nothing short of miraculous. The good news is that in a few years technology will be simpler to implement and access than ever before, making today's networks look like the room-sized, punchcard-spitting Univac computers of yore.

Turnkey technology will be ubiquitous in the world of work and will render flexibility so practical that it, too, will become pervasive. The pervasiveness of technology and its increasing simplification will be the driving force behind flexibility, rendering the conventional workplace obsolete and freeing us from the confines of the office cubicle.

Survival of the fittest — As individuals reap the rewards and contend with the challenges of increased family bonding and free time, what will the companies they work for be doing? Most will be thriving, as they harvest the fruits of increased productivity generated by a more loyal, more energized workforce. However, although we wish we could tell you that each and every company out there will adjust well to flexible employment, the truth is that some will not.

Mired in corporate cultures bogged down by convention and obsessed with the status quo, some companies will, alas, resist flexibility for far longer than is prudent. By the time these organizations attempt to catch up, we predict they will find many of their most talented employees working for more progressive competitors — and much of their own market share vanishing.

Winnowing-out is a natural if lamentable consequence of any major paradigm shift in society. In business, Darwin's rules of natural selection apply. Companies that adapt will thrive; those that don't will find themselves facing extinction.

Investing in a flexible future

Many people ask us what flexibility will mean for their personal investments down the road. Extrapolating from our predictions, they want to know if it's a good idea to invest in the companies providing goods and services that make sense in a world where the distinction between work life and home life won't be as clear as it is today. Our advice would be to invest in companies that are currently at the vanguard of the flexible employment movement.

What kinds of companies are pioneering flexible work arrangements? All kinds — new and old, small and large — including those in telecommunications, health care, biotechnology, banking, finance, insurance, pharmaceuticals, advertising, marketing, IT consulting, and e-commerce. The type of business is irrelevant. It's all about a type of thinking at the top that is open to embracing a new way of staffing.

Companies that embrace flexible staffing options as a matter of business policy are in a far better situation to weather economic ups and downs, since flexible staffing strategies help mitigate the typical cycle of bloated salaries followed by layoffs. These are the companies that have the best chance of retaining their top people and the best chance of attracting the next generation of talent, which will demand flexibility in ever-increasing numbers. They are the companies whose staffing strategies will ripple throughout the world, because they produce goods and services with employees who are energized, focused, motivated, and have a strong sense of loyalty to employers that allow them the work/life balance necessary for their well-being. Companies that invest in non-traditional staffing policies for business reasons — reasons that make the most bottom-line sense — will also flourish, for all of these reasons.

In fact, organizations that have already embraced flexibility and are actively planning to expand their flexible employment programs in the coming years are going to do very well indeed as the rest of the decade unfolds. They are the ones that are — and will be — delivering the best service to their customers. They are the ones that will attract and retain the best and the brightest. Ultimately, they are the companies that embody both the optimism and the pragmatism essential for success in the 21st century.

End Notes

CHAPTER 1

1. As cited in "Flexible and Non-Standard Hours and Employment Arrangements: An Overview of Current Trends and Patterns," presented by Lonnie Golden, Ph.D. at the 12th annual meeting of the International Society for Work Options, April 1999.

2. Lewis, Michael, *The New New Thing: A Silicon Valley Story*, (New York: Norton, 2000), p. 169.

3. "A Game of Nerves, With No Real Winner," *The New York Times*, May 17, 2000, p. H1.

4. Gleick, James, *Faster: The Acceleration of Just About Everything*, (New York: Pantheon, 1999), p. 122.

5. "Talking About Tomorrow," *The Wall Street Journal*, January 1, 2000, p. R16.

CHAPTER 2

1. "For Harried Workers in the 21st Century, Six Trends to Watch," *The Wall Street Journal*, December 29, 1999, p. B1.

2. *Business Week*, September 20, 1999.

3. "The Secret Wild Card: Employees Want Jobs That Help Caregivers," *The Wall Street Journal*, June 14, 2000, p. B1.

4. "The Retirement Lobby Goes Va-Va-Boom," *The New York Times*, August 8, 1999, *Week in Review*, p. 1.

5. "Older People Want to Work in Retirement, Survey Finds," *The New York Times*, September 2, 1999, p. A18.

6. "Young Male Workers Put Family First," *The Wilmington Star-News*, May 7, 2000, p. E1. (Reprinted from *The Washington Post*)

7. Ibid.

8. Thurow, Lester, *Building Wealth: The New Rules for Individuals, Companies and Nations*, (New York: Harper Collins, 1999).

9. As cited in "The Integration of Worklife with Other HR Issues," presented by Vivian Jarcho, Human Resources Manager, U.S. Dept of Justice, at the 12th annual meeting of the International Society for Work Options, April 1999.

CHAPTER 3

1. Olmstead, Barney and Smith, Suzanne, *Creating a Flexible Workplace: How to Select and Manage Alternative Work Options* (New York: Amacom, 1989), pp. 12-13.

2. Ibid, p. 106.

3. "Job Sharing Working Its Way Into Mainstream," *The Chicago Tribune*, August 1, 2000, p. B1.

4. "Rise of the Permatemp," *Time*, July 12, 1999.

5. Peters, Tom, *The Brand You 50*, (New York: Knopf, 1999).

6. Regan was quoted in "Meet the Future," *Fortune*, July 24, 2000.

7. "Los Alamos Lab Tries to Stem the Decline of Bomb Know-How," *The Wall Street Journal*, August 2, 2000, p. 1.

8. The four cities in our survey were Boston, New York, San Francisco and Los Angeles. The respondent base is a sufficiently

large sample to represent an accurate picture of the entire candidate population. The results reflect the population within a statistical range of +/-5%.

9. "Forget the Raise, Give Me Some Time Off," *The New York Times*, July 12, 2000, p. G1.

CHAPTER 4

1. From Abraham Lincoln's address on 22 Feb. 1842 to the Washingtonian Temperance Society in Springfield, Illinois.

CHAPTER 5

1. "Memo to Staff: Stop Working," *The Wall Street Journal*, July 6, 2000, p. B1.

2. Ibid.

3. Ibid.

4. "The Basic Principles of Civility Cubed," *The New York Times*, October 4, 2000, p. G1.

5. Harvard Business Review, *Harvard Business Review on Work and Life Balance*, (Boston: Harvard Business School Press, 2000), p. 148.

CHAPTER 6

1. The advisory was actually posted to OSHA's Web site on November 15, but did not draw media attention and public furor until January 2000.

2. Associated Press wire report, 2:34 p.p. EST, January 5, 2000.

3. "Business Groups Attack OSHA Advisory," *The Wall Street Journal*, January 5, 2000.

4. "Working At Home Today?" *The New York Times*, November 2, 2000, p. G1.

5. *SoHo Today*, October 20, 2000, p.10.

6. "Work and Family," *The Wall Street Journal*, November 15, 2000, p. B1.

7. "Working At Home Today?" *The New York Times*, Op Cit.

CHAPTER 7

1. "Fighting Sleep on the Job? Join the Crowd," *The New York Times*, February 5, 2001, p. G1.

2. "I'll Be Right With You, Boss, As Soon As I Finish My Shopping," *The New York Times*, January 10, 2001, p. G1.

3. *Time*, July 24, 2000, p. 23.

CHAPTER 8

1. Op cit. 1999 survey by the Society of Human Resource Management (SHRM).

2. The MBTI is available from Consulting Psychologists Press.

CHAPTER 9

1. "HBR Case Study," *The Harvard Business Review*, March, 2001, pp. 33-42.

CHAPTER 10

1. Sampson, Anthony, *Company Man*, (New York: Crown, 1995), p. 63.

2. Howard, Philip K., *The Lost Art of Drawing the Line*, (New York: Random House, 2001), pp. 83-86.

3. "Companies Must Try Harder to Attract Older Employees," *The Wall Street Journal*, May 23, 2001, p. C1.

4. "No Time to Put Your Feet Up as Retirement Comes in Stages," *The New York Times*, April 15, 2000, p. A1.

0-595-21735-4